THE
NEW YORKER
BOOK OF TECHNOLOGY CARTOONS

THE
NEW YORKER
BOOK OF
TECHNOLOGY CARTOONS

EDITED AND WITH AN INTRODUCTION BY ROBERT MANKOFF
IN ASSOCIATION WITH CARTOONBANK.COM

BLOOMBERG PRESS

NEW YORK

PUBLISHED BY BLOOMBERG PRESS

First edition published 2000
Reprinted in 2007

1 3 5 7 9 10 8 6 4 2

Library of Congress Cataloging-in-Publication Data

The New Yorker book of technology cartoons / edited and with an introduction by
Robert Mankoff in association with Cartoonbank.com. — 1st ed.
    p. cm.
  Originally published: 2000.
  Includes index.
  ISBN 978-1-57660-313-0 (alk. paper)
  1. Technology—Caricatures and cartoons. 2. American wit and humor, Pictorial.
I. Mankoff, Robert. II. New Yorker (New York, N.Y. : 1925) III.
Title: Book of technology cartoons.

NC1763.T42N49 2007
741.5'356—dc22   2007060593

Book design by LAURIE LOHNE / Design It Communications

THE
NEW YORKER
BOOK OF TECHNOLOGY CARTOONS

*W*elcome to the Introduction to 'The New Yorker *Book of Technology Cartoons*'

Please press any key to continue.

ALERT! Error Code—006#!%!!—No Key Pressed—Human Error—You. That's right, you. We know all about you. Our sophisticated tracking technology has been sending us your data ever since you purchased this book. And everything seemed OK until you refused to press that key. Now it appears you have an antitechnological tendency that has to be dealt with. My advice: get over it, move on—technology already has.

The essence of technology is change. In fact, the world of technology changes so fast that by the time you finish this introduction the first part of it will already be obsolete. Fortunately, an upgrade is already available and can be downloaded at www.bythetimeyoufinishthisintroductionthefirstpartofitwillbe-obsolete.com or at its mirror site: moɔ.ətɘloɛdoɔɘdlliwɈiʇoɈɹɒqɈɛɹiʇɘɖɈnoiɈɔubσɹɈni-ɛiɖɈɖɛiniʇuoγɘmiɈɘɖɈγd.www.

If downloading the upgrade fails, upgrading your download software may be required. However, if that exceeds the meager bandwidth of your wetware, versions of the introduction's upgrade are also available offline at fine NotDot-Com stores everywhere in CD, DVD, and the increasingly popular BVD formats (S, M, L, or XL).

As you may have guessed by now, I'm a technophile. Look, it could be worse. I could be a Francophile. Actually, it's more complicated than that; I have a love-hate relationship with technology—I love it when it works, and I hate it when it doesn't. But even when the technology works, I often find myself resenting it. Like when my communications center tells me I have no voice mail, no pager messages, no e-mail, and no friends. Or when my Global Positioning System, which is constantly tracking my exact spot on Earth to within fifty feet, suggests that really, I should get out more. Or when my computer cannot find a chess level low enough to play with me and recommends a "smart" appliance as a suitable opponent. (Or when the appliance wins.) At moments like these I find myself quickly changing from a mild-mannered technophile to a wild-mannered technopath.

But these technocidal impulses never hold sway for long. And before you can say "dot-com," I'm plunging ever deeper into a world where Murphy's Law combines with Moore's Law to insure that everything that can go wrong will go wrong, but at twice the rate that it did eighteen months ago. Example: I've got a new electronic organizer clipped right on the back of my cell phone. And the phone has been tweaked to function as a wireless modem for my laptop, which can now transfer e-mails back to my organizer, which, of course, causes it to run out of memory. Now, I could get more memory for the organizer, or I could wait for the next product cycle to spawn an updated version that could handle the increased message load. This new organizer would undoubtedly require me to replace all the other equipment in my high-tech scheme, but frankly, it's about time I got rid of all that old junk anyway.

The absurdity of all this is not lost on me. As soon as I put my e-check in the e-mail for the latest e-thing I'm thinking, "Egad! I've become desperately dependent on an army of devices that I don't need." It makes me wonder: if, as all the information-age pundits tell me, technology is my servant, how come I've become its slave?

I'd like to place the blame for all this on the new economy, the new media, the new paradigm, or that new e-thing I just bought, but the real culprit is just plain old me, as this fifteen-year-old, very autobiographical *New Yorker* cartoon of mine attests.

"All my gadgets are old. I'd like some new gadgets."

Basically, I never met a consumer technology I didn't like. You build it, and I'll buy it. Why? Well, if this pocket genome decoder of mine is correct, it's because I'm hardwired for it.

Other cartoonists are wired a bit differently. The ones in this book represent a continuum with me over at one end (some would say the deep end) while on the other end are guys like Charlie Barsotti and Jack Ziegler, who view any technology later than that of the technical pen with suspicion. Although they use computers and their ilk, their attitude, as expressed in the self-portraits done for this introduction, is that the computers are using *them.*

Charles Barsotti   Jack Ziegler

But if Ziegler and Barsotti think that a cartoonist needs cutting-edge technology as much as a fish needs a bicycle, Tom (Borg) Cheney clearly envisions a day when a bioengineered flounder wins the Tour de France.

Tom Cheney

Other self-portraits, like those of Mick Stevens and Marisa Acocella, evince a vague sense of foreboding, bringing to mind Yeats's prophetic quote from *The Second Coming,* "Turning and turning in the widening gyre / The falcon cannot hear the falconer; / Nor can he page him." Acocella's drawing further suggests the question "If this is the information age, how come we can't retain any?"

Mick Stevens

Marisa Acocella

In fact, I happen to know the answer to *that* question. Or at least I know the database the answer is stored in. Now, if only I could remember the password. Clearly, we have become dependent on technology. We can't live without it. How it feels about us, however, is another matter addressed by the one cartoonist I know who actually draws his cartoons on a computer.

Alex Gregory

Gregory may be right. Time is running out for cartoons done by humans, or even looked at by humans. But don't despair, the carbon-based life-form is still in the driver's seat, even though—as Frank Cotham's portrait shows—it's getting a little crowded up there.

Frank Cotham

Meanwhile, my advice is to enjoy the ride, no matter how bumpy. The jokes are on us, about us, and for us, and all you have to do to access 110 of them is to press any key below.

On second thought, just turn the page.

"You've got mail."

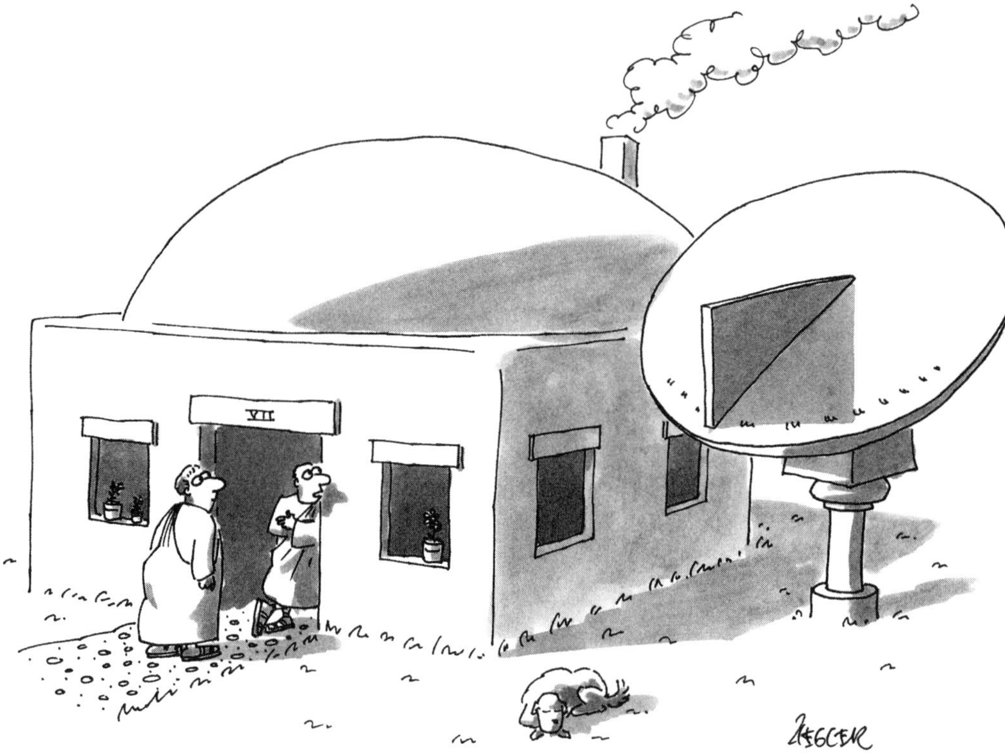
VII

"Sure, it's an eyesore, but we get better time than anyone else in the neighborhood."

"First, they do an on-line search."

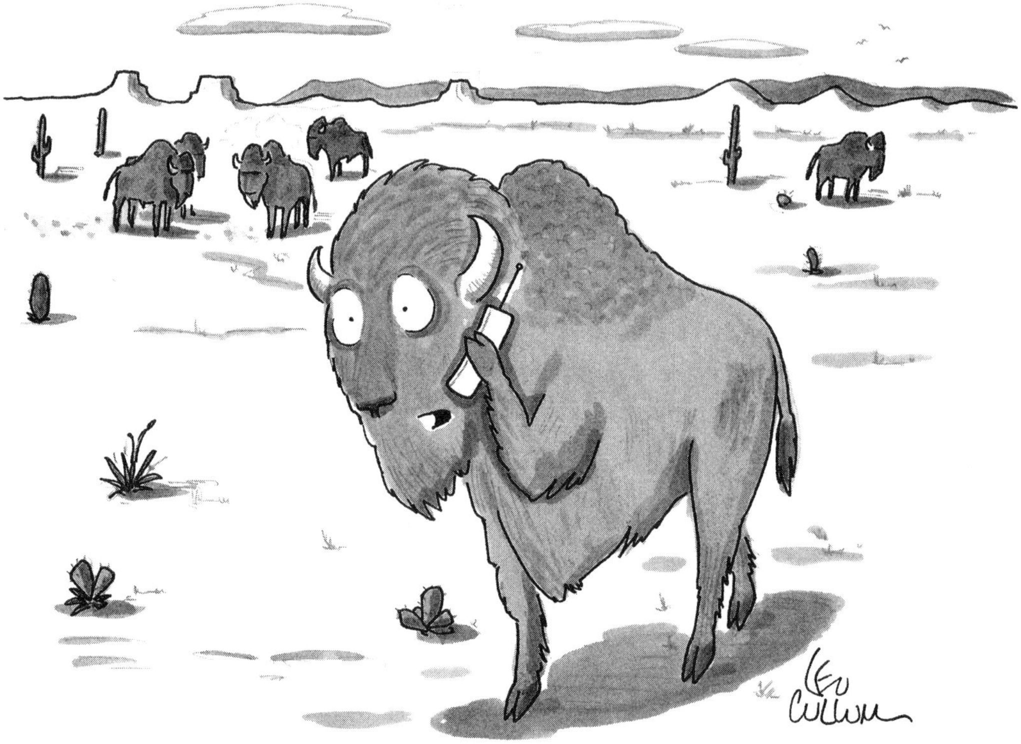
LEO CULLUM

"I love the convenience, but the roaming charges are killing me."

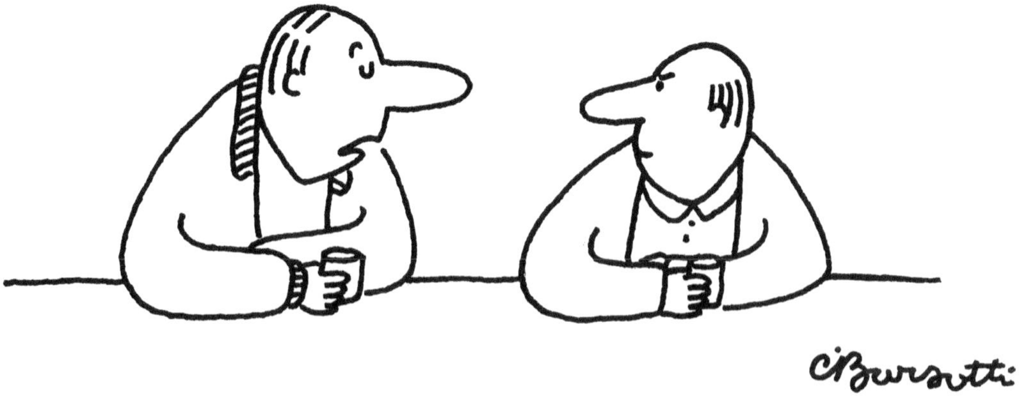
CBarsotti

"Oh, like you know something the Internet doesn't know."

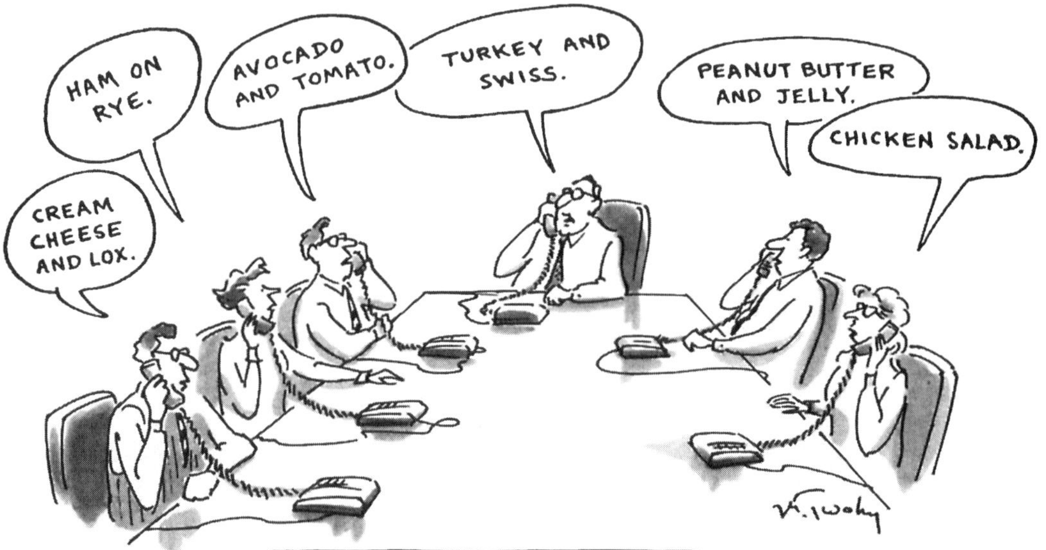
HAM ON RYE.
CREAM CHEESE AND LOX.
AVOCADO AND TOMATO.
TURKEY AND SWISS.
PEANUT BUTTER AND JELLY.
CHICKEN SALAD.

CONFERENCE CALL

"I'm sorry, Mr. Abbot is away from his desk."

SIPRESS

"Keep your eyes on your own screen."

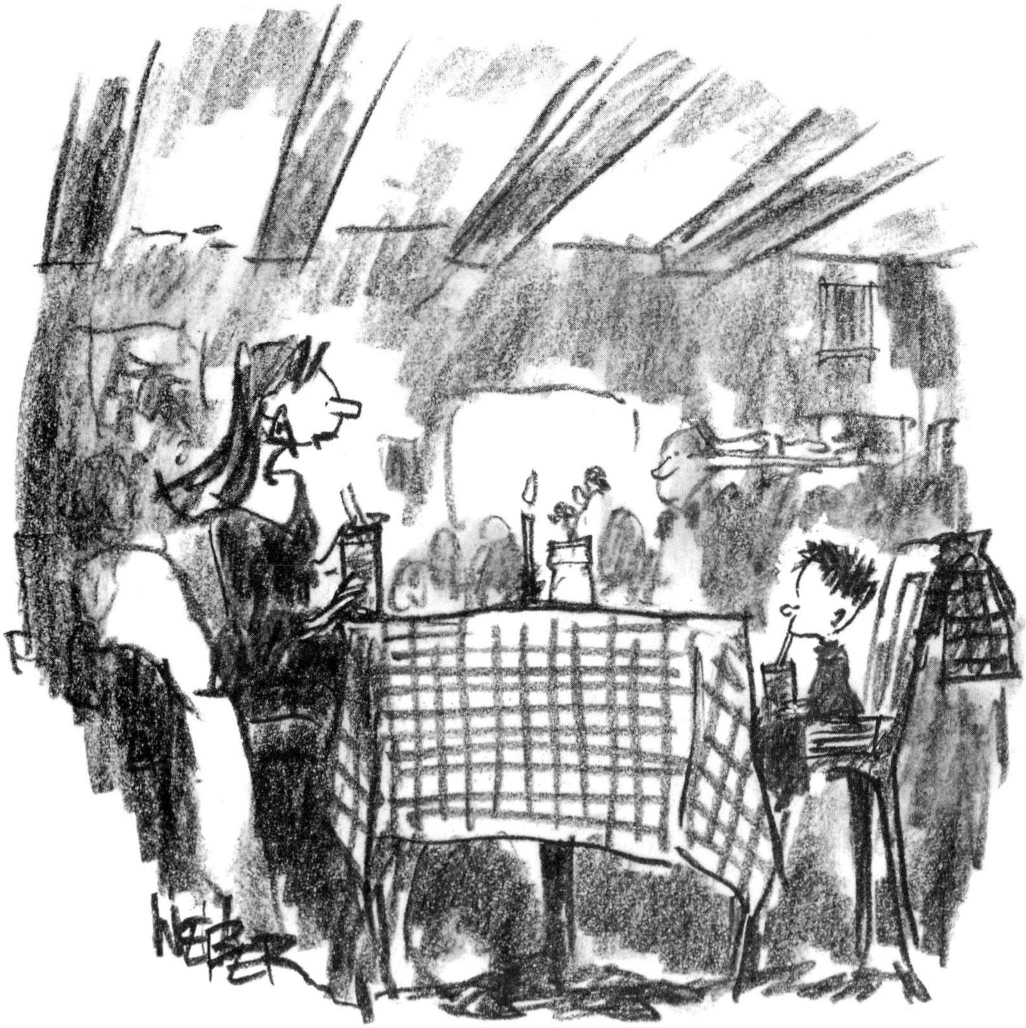
WEBER

"I loved your E-mail, but I thought you'd be older."

INFORMATION-AGE LOSERS

THE I.R.S. CHANNEL

INTERACTIVE WELDING

VIRTUAL VIDEO

"All I'm saying is <u>now</u> is the time to develop the technology to deflect an asteroid."

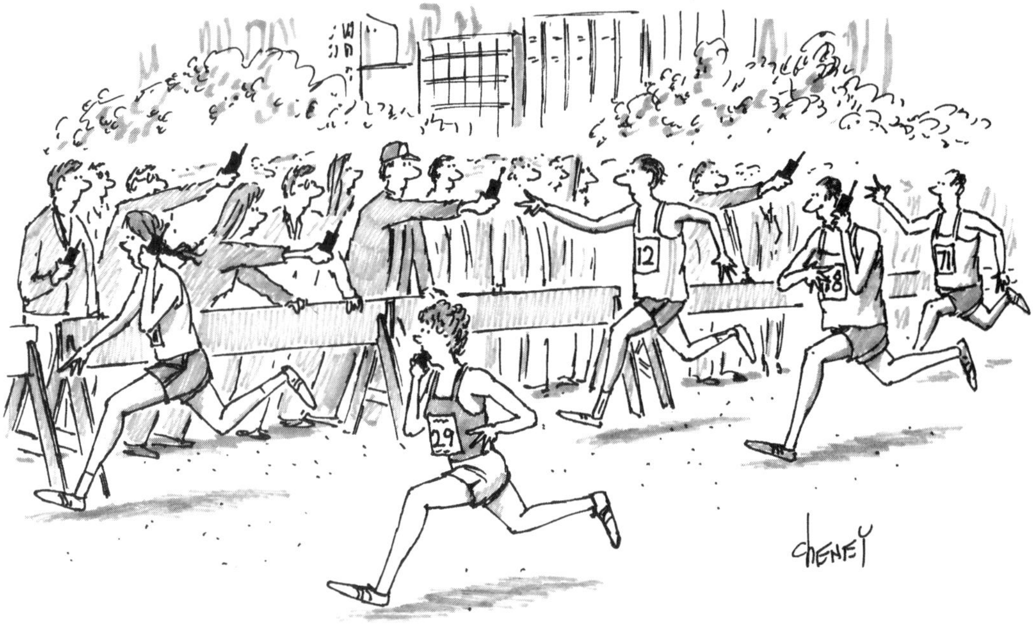
12
71
29
CHENEY

"*You see that dark, spooky image on the screen? That's your credit history coming back to haunt you.*"

"You can access me by saying simply 'Agnes.' It is not necessary to add 'dot com.'"

"Hello. I'm a first-time caller."

"We are all fed up with you
doing these damn power breakfasts at home."

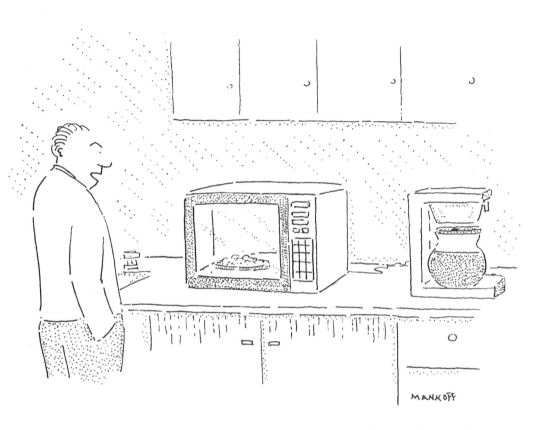

"No, I don't want to play chess. I just want you to reheat the lasagna."

"And then I met some computer people who could make it look as if I were talking."

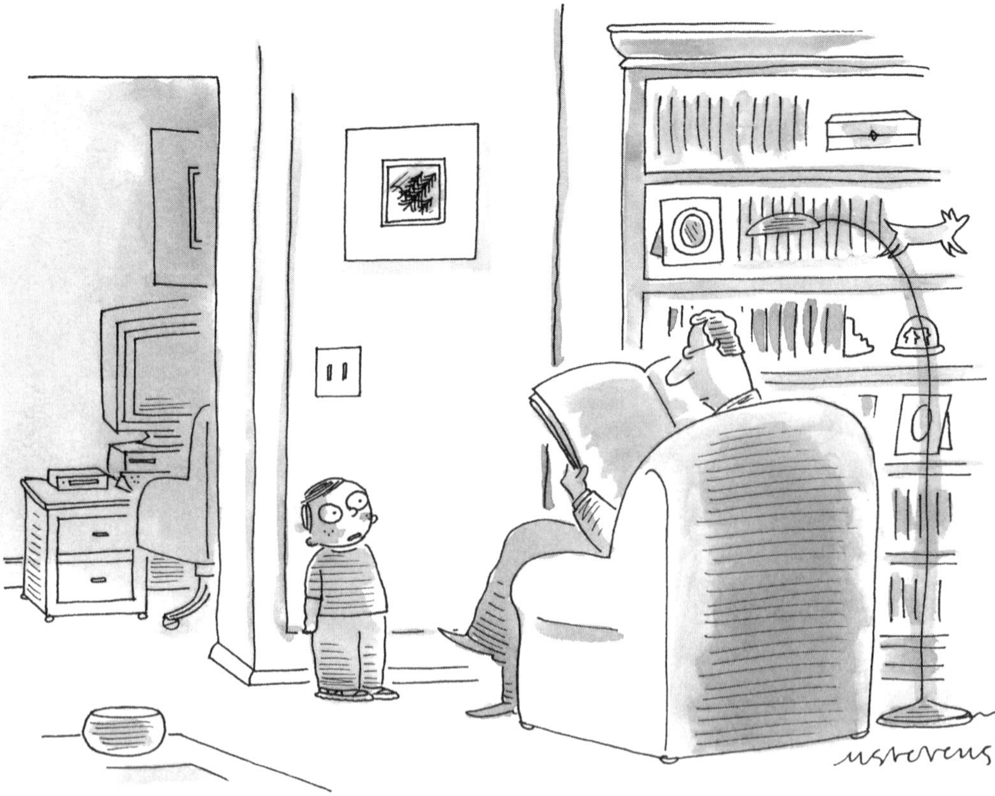
MStevens

"Dad, can I borrow your password tonight?"

"It must be his beeper."

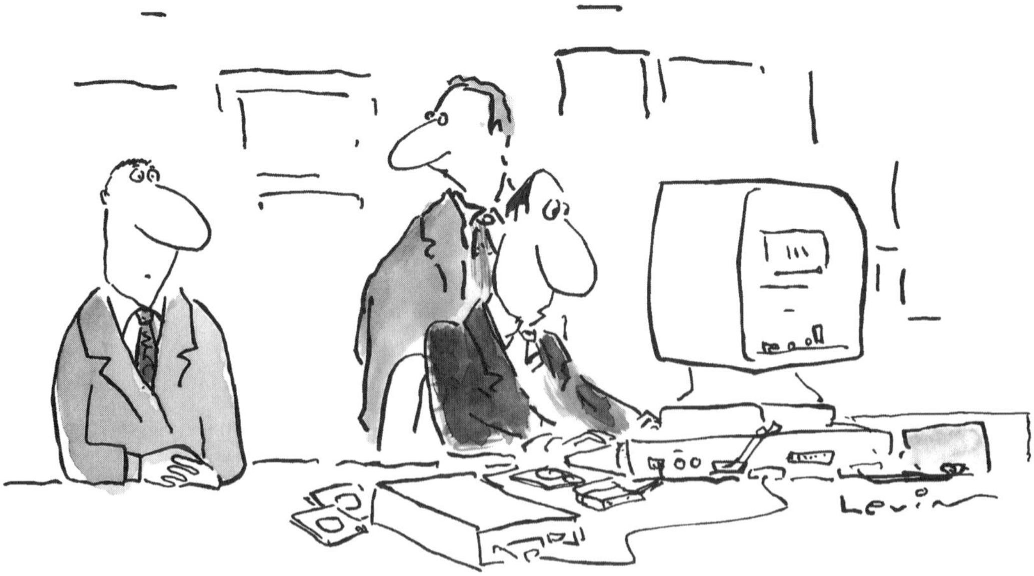
LEVIN

"I haven't the slightest idea who he is. He came bundled with the software."

"From right to left, you have your tekkamaki, your futomaki, and then your yamaimo roll. The little pile of pink stuff is ginger, the green one's wasabi. And, of course, you already recognize your vodka martini."

"Alright, Ms. Ramsey, send in the clones."

"The gods must be on-line tonight."

"Nothing important—nothing on fax, nothing on voice mail, nothing on the Internet. Just, you know, handwritten stuff."

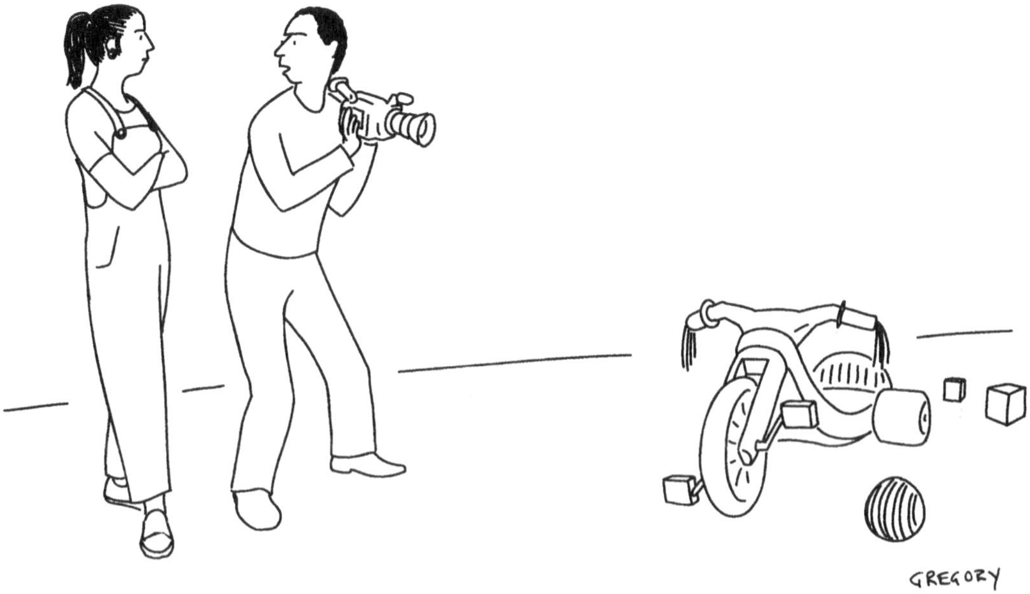
GREGORY

"I figure we can blue-screen the kids in later."

"If there is anyone who objects to this union, either here or on
the Internet, speak now or forever hold your peace."

"Well, being single and a robot, I'm able to put in a lot of overtime."

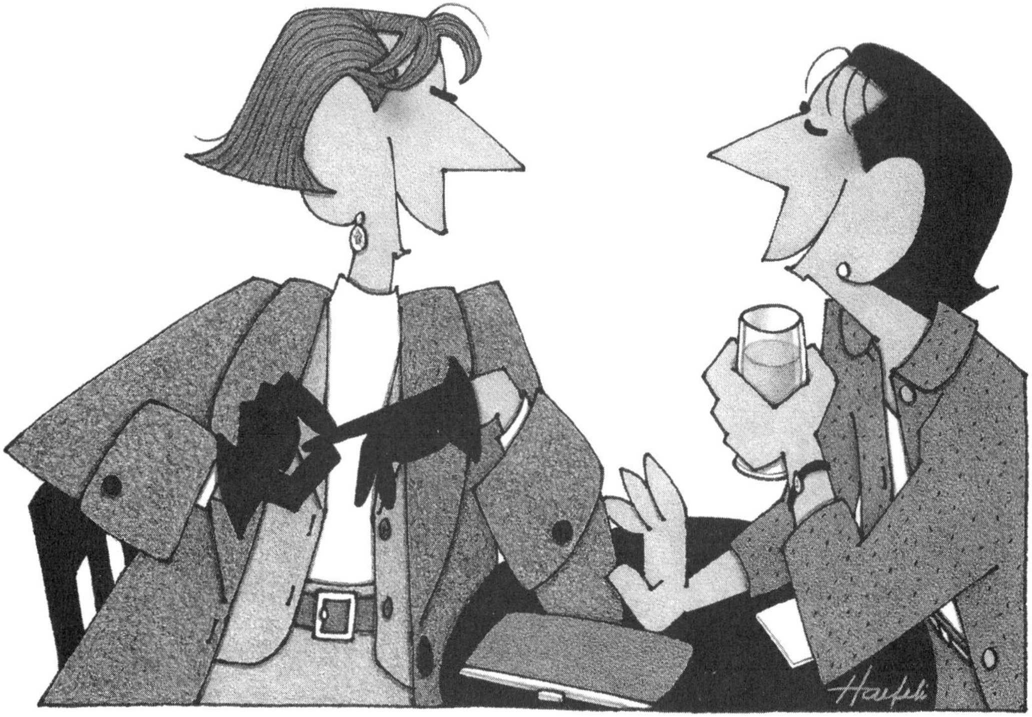
Haefeli

"I sold his unlisted phone number to telemarketers."

"Just for kicks, Leon, let's shut down the F.B.I. again."

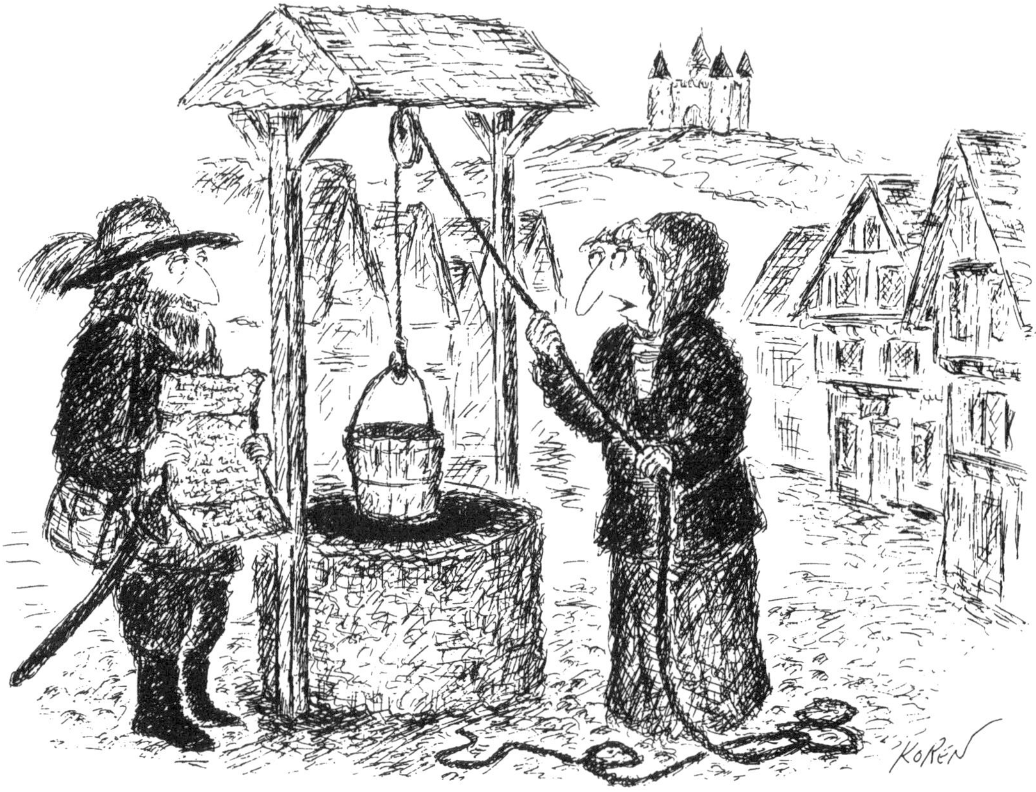
KOREN

"First, let me pull up your file."

"Very nice résumé. Leave a sample of your DNA with my secretary."

"This is so cool! I'm flying this thing completely on my Palm pilot!"

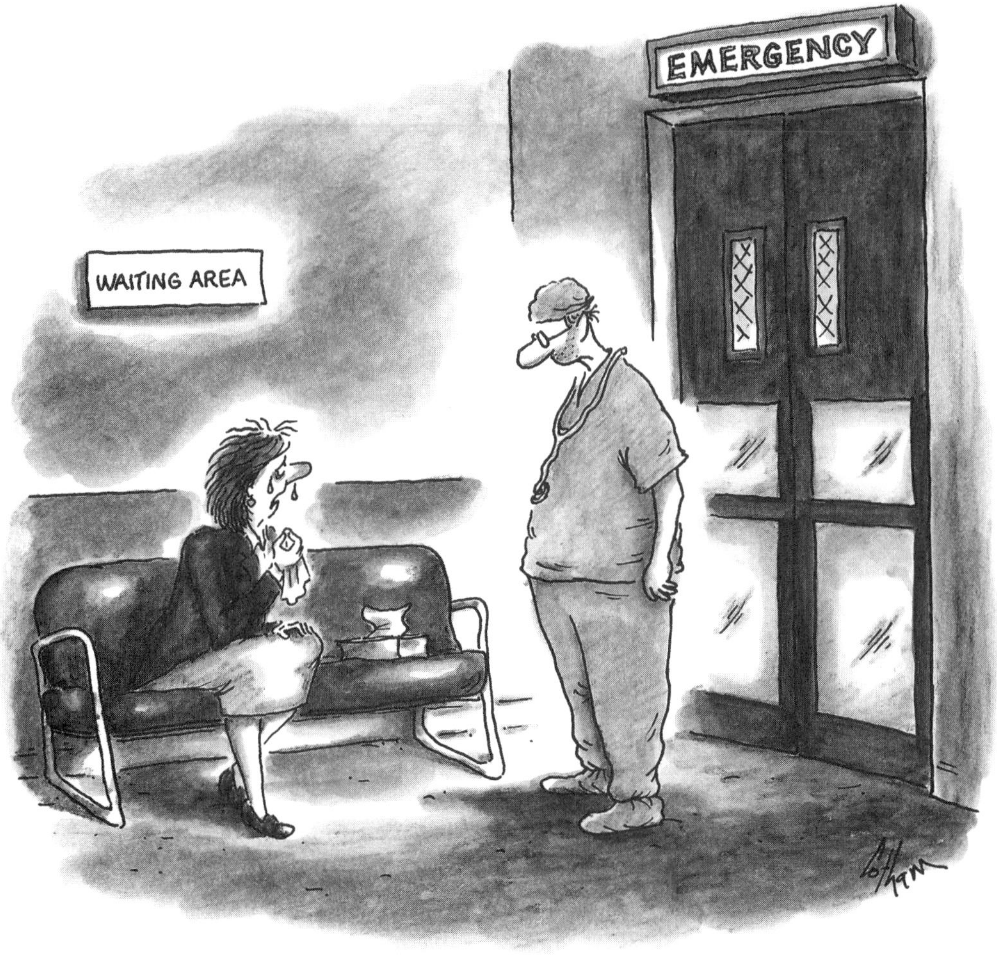
EMERGENCY
WAITING AREA

"I already know he's gone—it's been on the Internet."

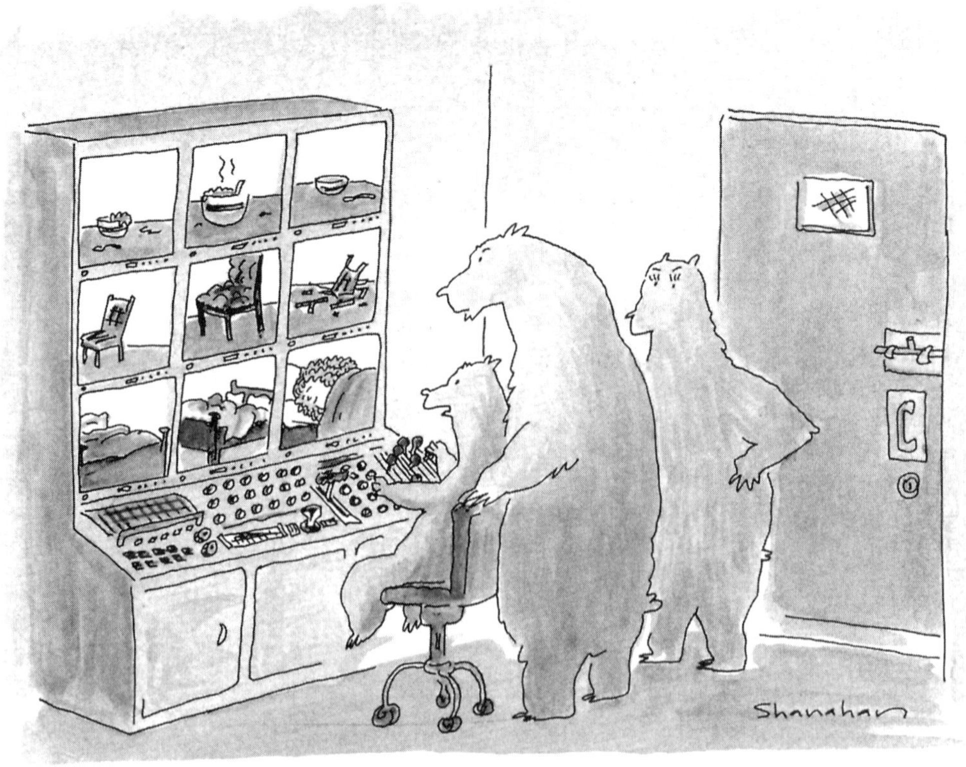
Shanahan

"Someone's been sleeping in my bed, too, and there she is on Screen Nine!"

"*You are entitled to one call, one fax, or one e-mail.*"

"Can I call you back? I'm shopping."

"Are we thinking here, or is this just so much pointing and clicking?"

Please listen carefully, as my menu options have changed."

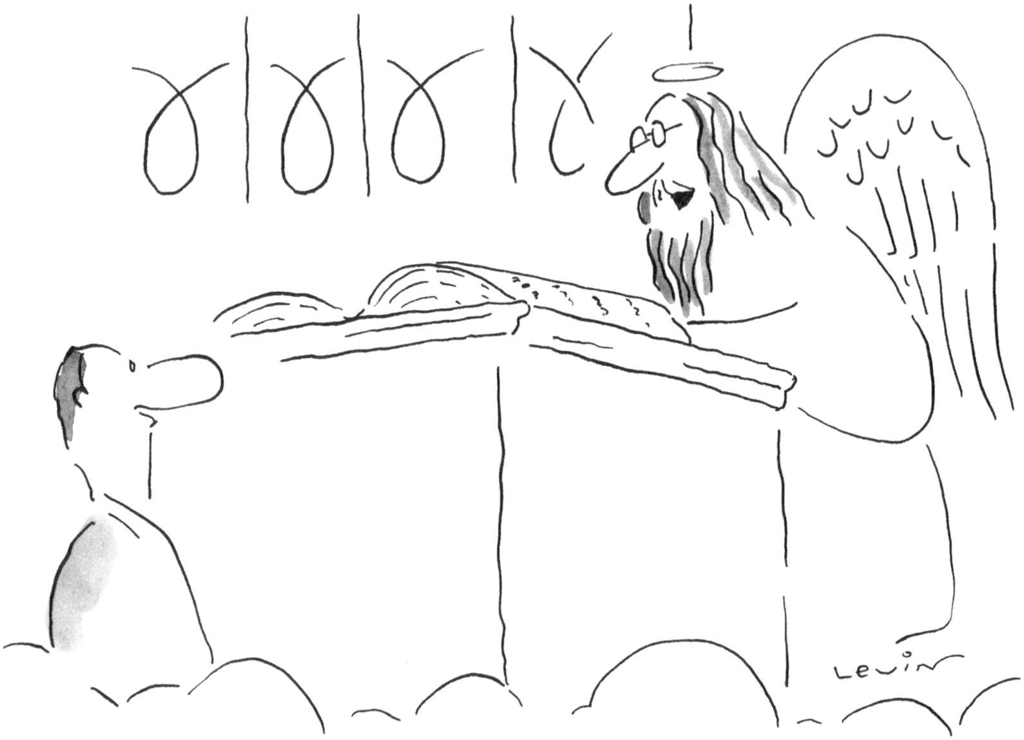
LEVIN

"User name and password?"

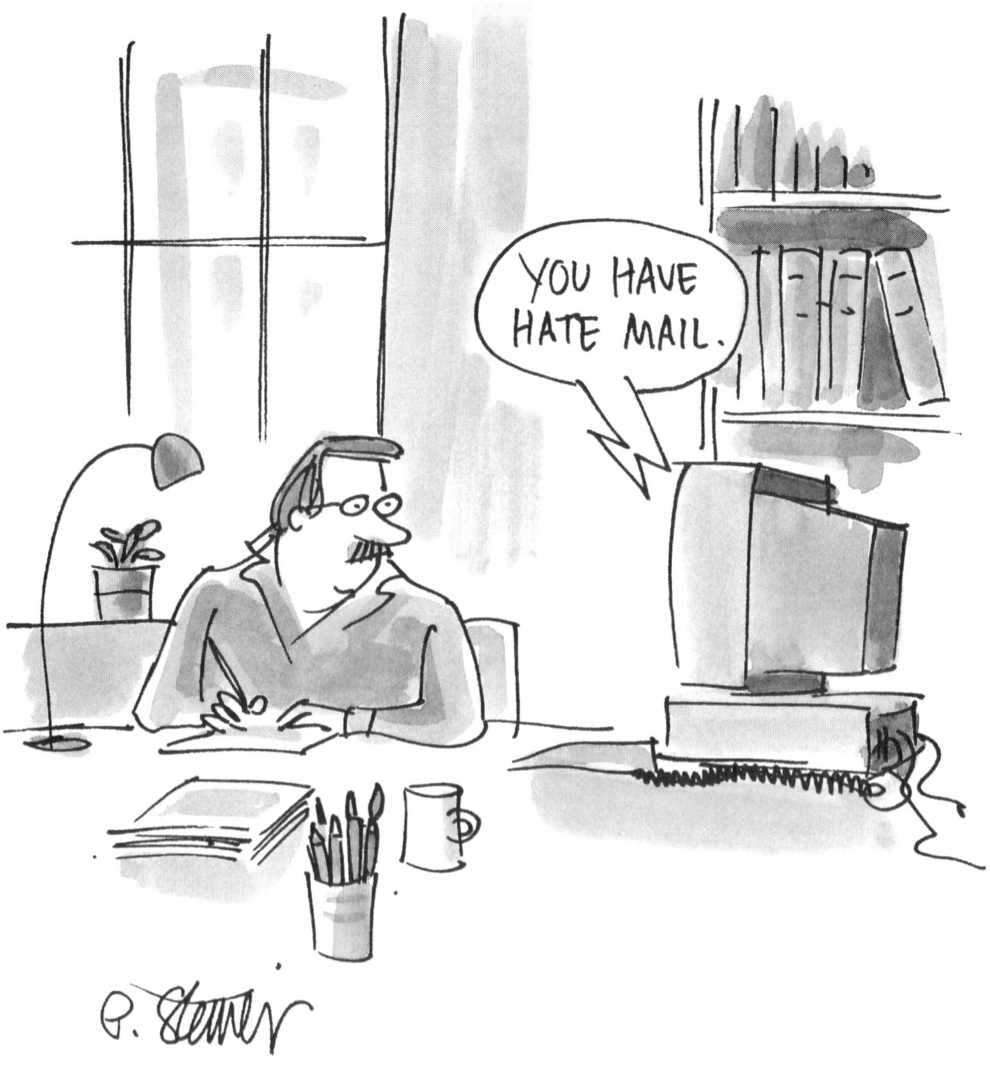
YOU HAVE HATE MAIL.

"Oh, Lord! We forgot to invite any content providers."

"Marry me, Virginia. My genes are excellent and, as yet, unpatented."

AMERICA OFF-LINE

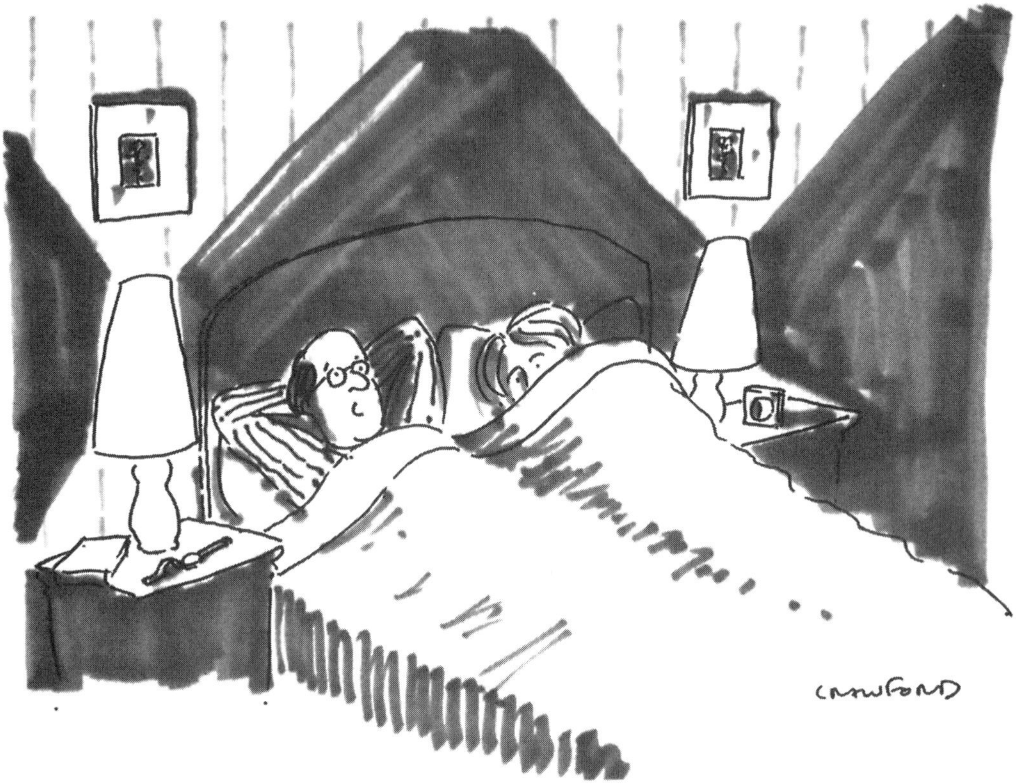
CRAWFORD

"Not tonight, hon. It'll just wreak havoc with the motion sensors again."

"Trust me Mort—no electronic-communications superhighway, no matter how vast and sophisticated, will ever replace the art of the schmooze."

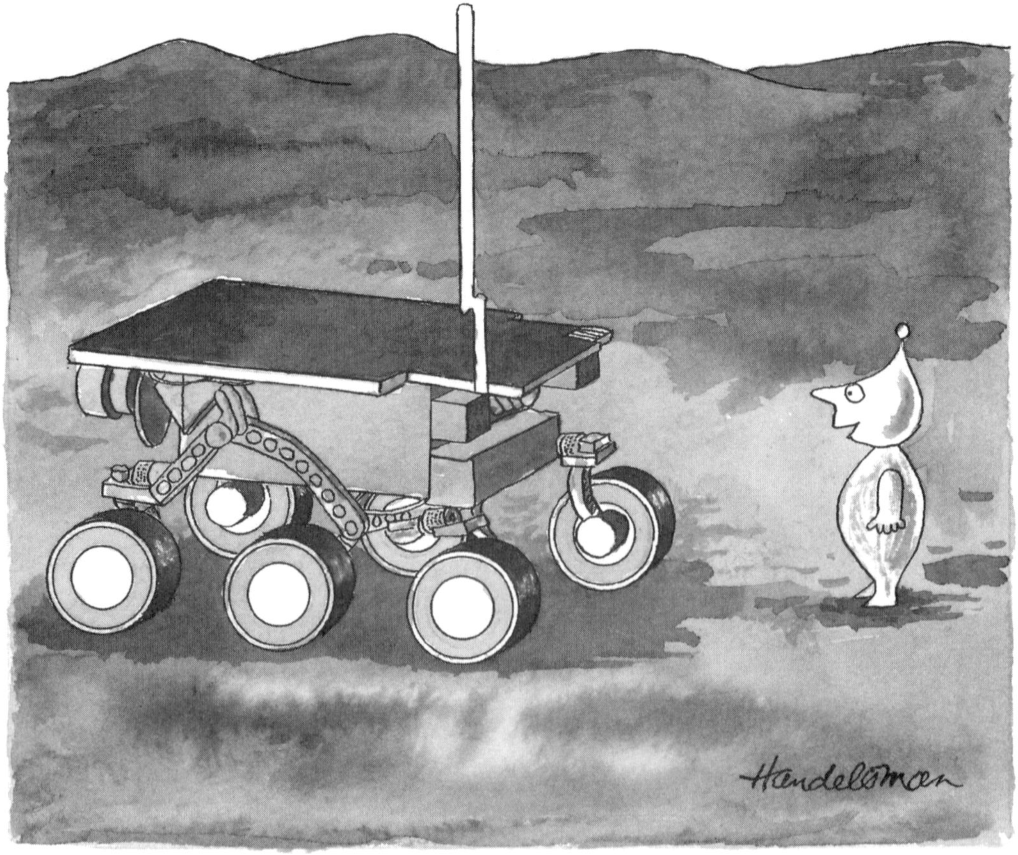
Handelsman

"I'd like to say 'Hi' to my granddaddy in Roswell, New Mexico."

PERPETRATOR OF A DARING DAYLIGHT ILLEGAL ELECTRONIC TRANSFER OF FUNDS FLEEING THE SCENE OF THE CRIME

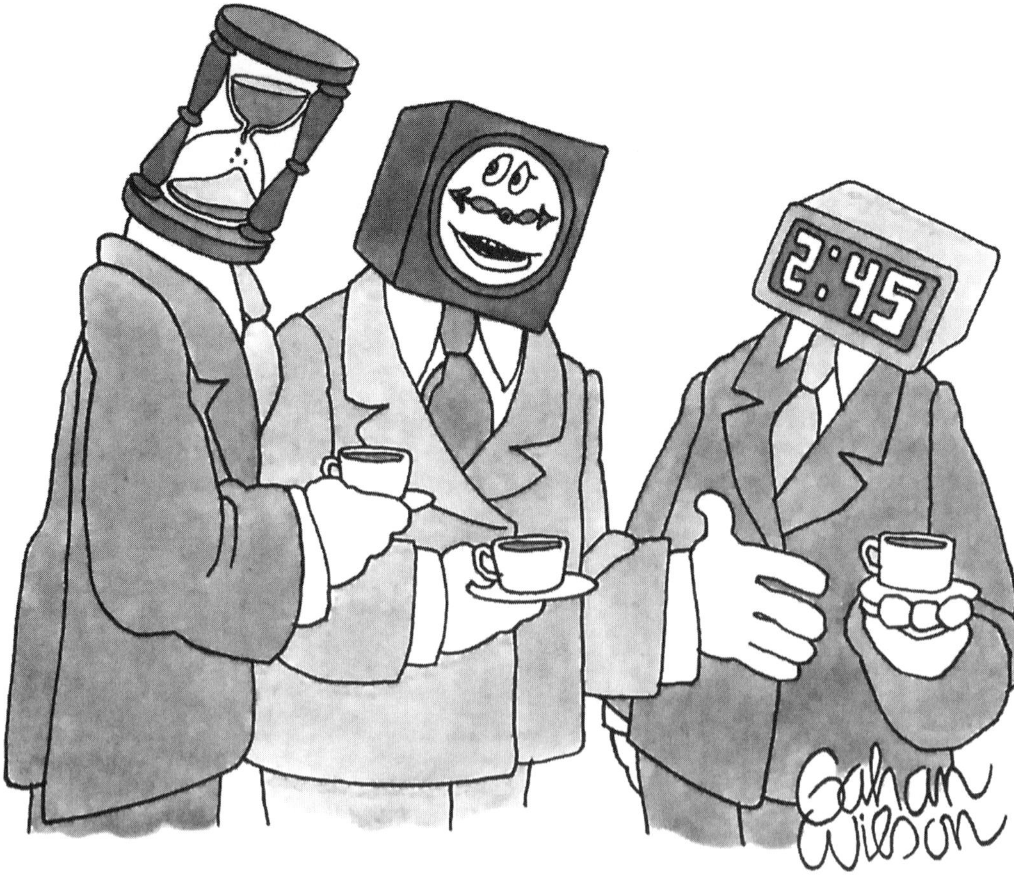
2:45
Gahan Wilson

"Basically, we're all trying to say the same thing."

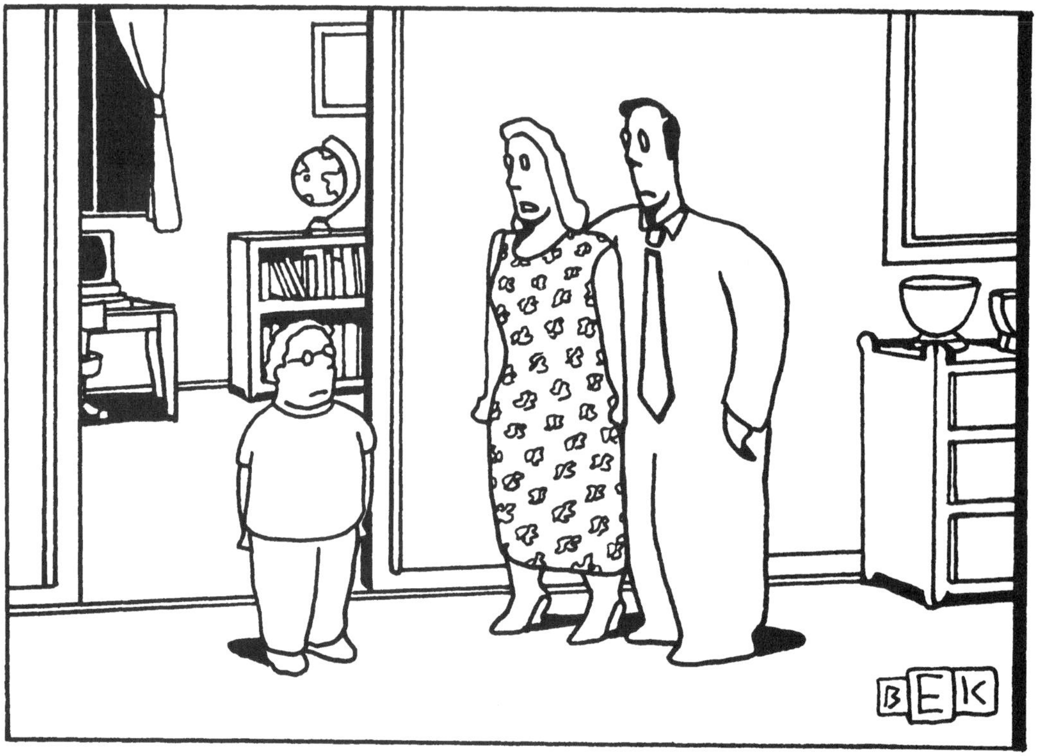
BEK

"We're neither software nor hardware. We're your parents."

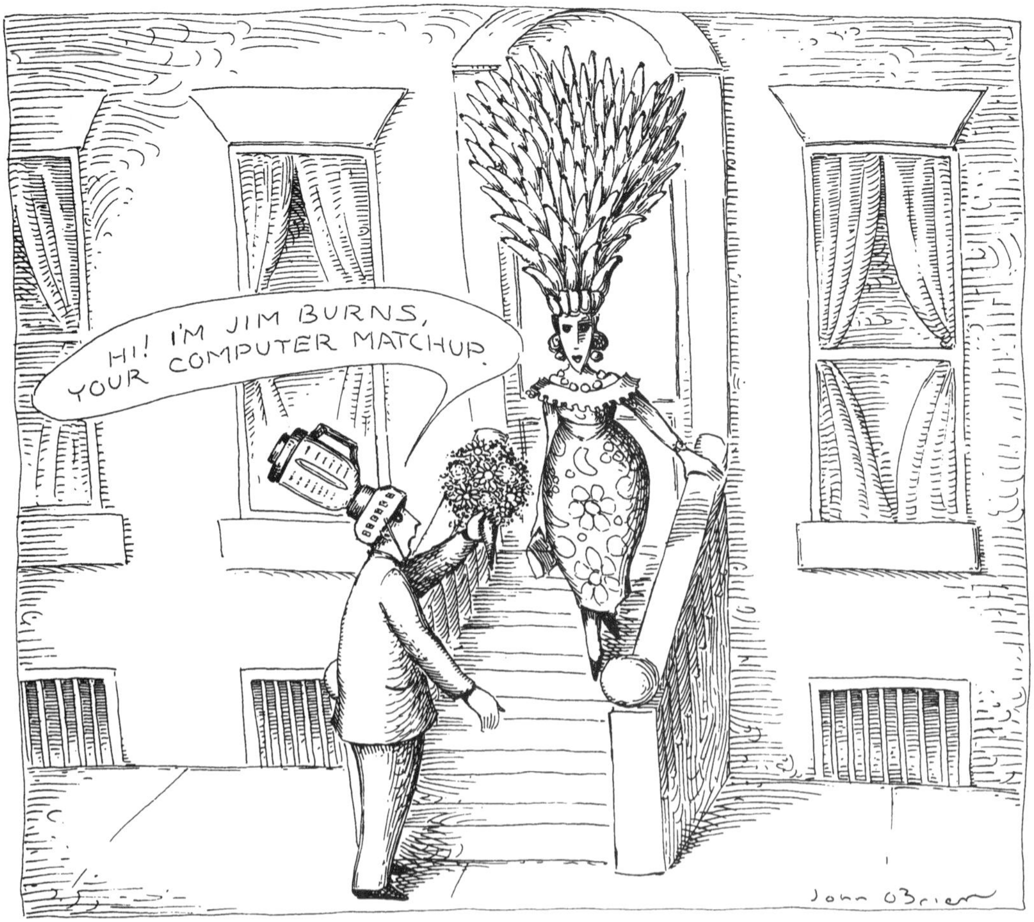
HI! I'M JIM BURNS, YOUR COMPUTER MATCHUP.
John O'Brien

"When we implant your pacemaker, we can, for a modest
additional fee, also implant your beeper."

"Thank you very much, but I'm more than satisfied
with my present long-distance carrier."

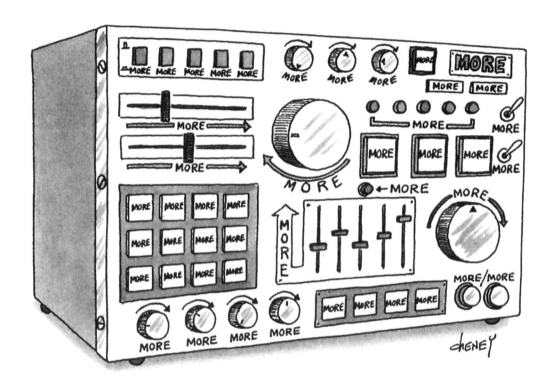

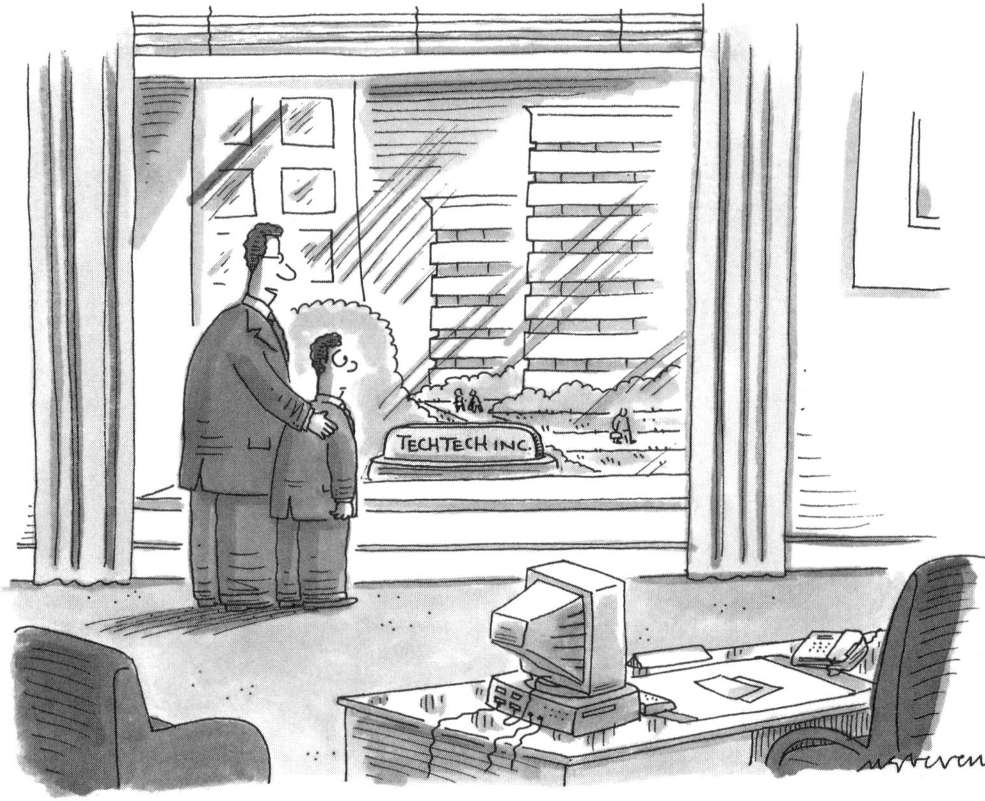
TECHTECH INC.

"Someday, son, all this will belong to Bill Gates."

"What about that! His brain still uses the old vacuum tubes."

"I'm delighted to love, honor, and obey, but I'm keeping my electronic rights."

"*You say you love me, but I'm not on your speed dial.*"

"On the Internet, nobody knows you're a dog."

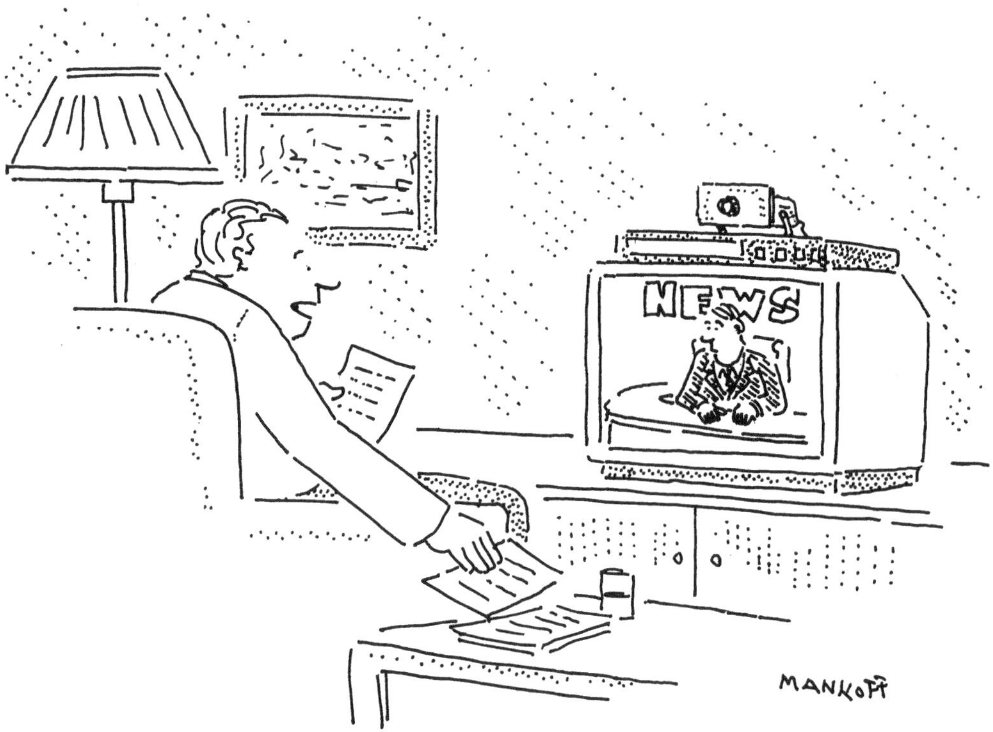
NEWS
MANKOFF

"The much ballyhooed era of TV interactivity took a step closer to reality today."

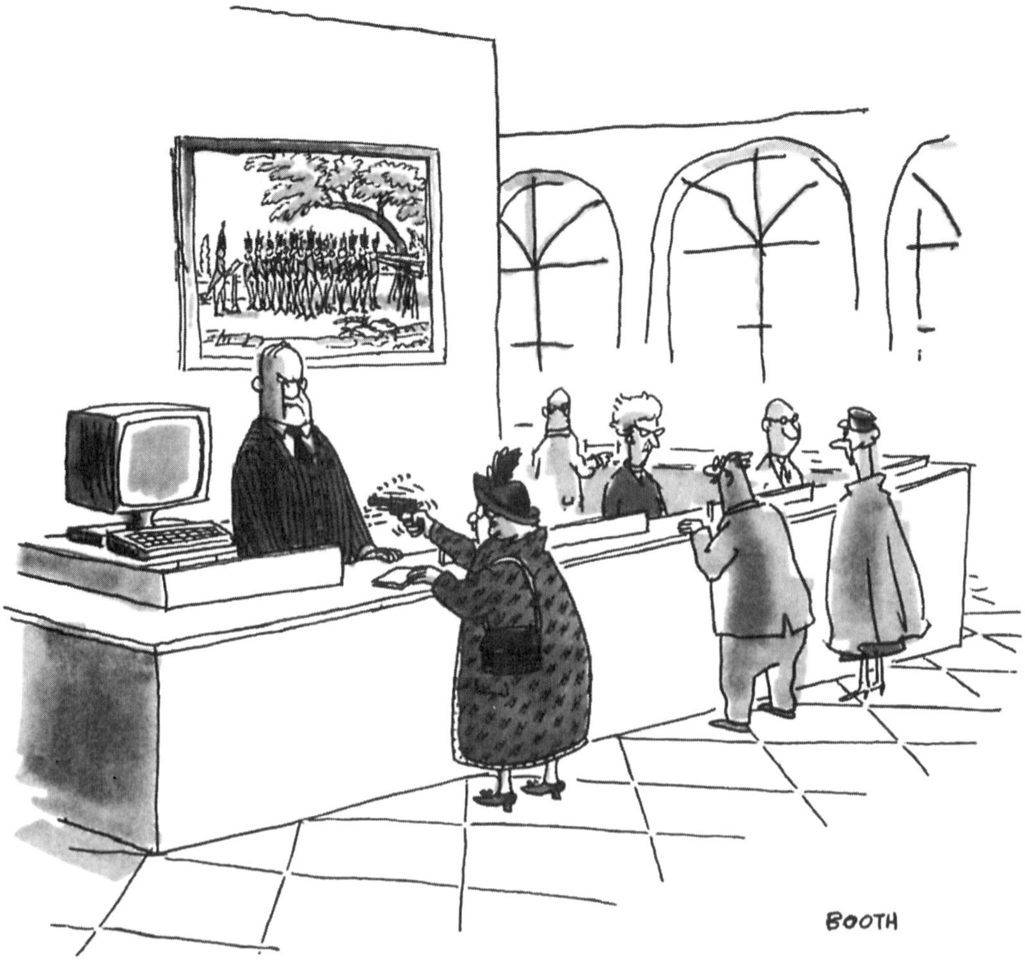
BOOTH

"Stand aside, Gruenwald! It's the computer I'm blowing away!"

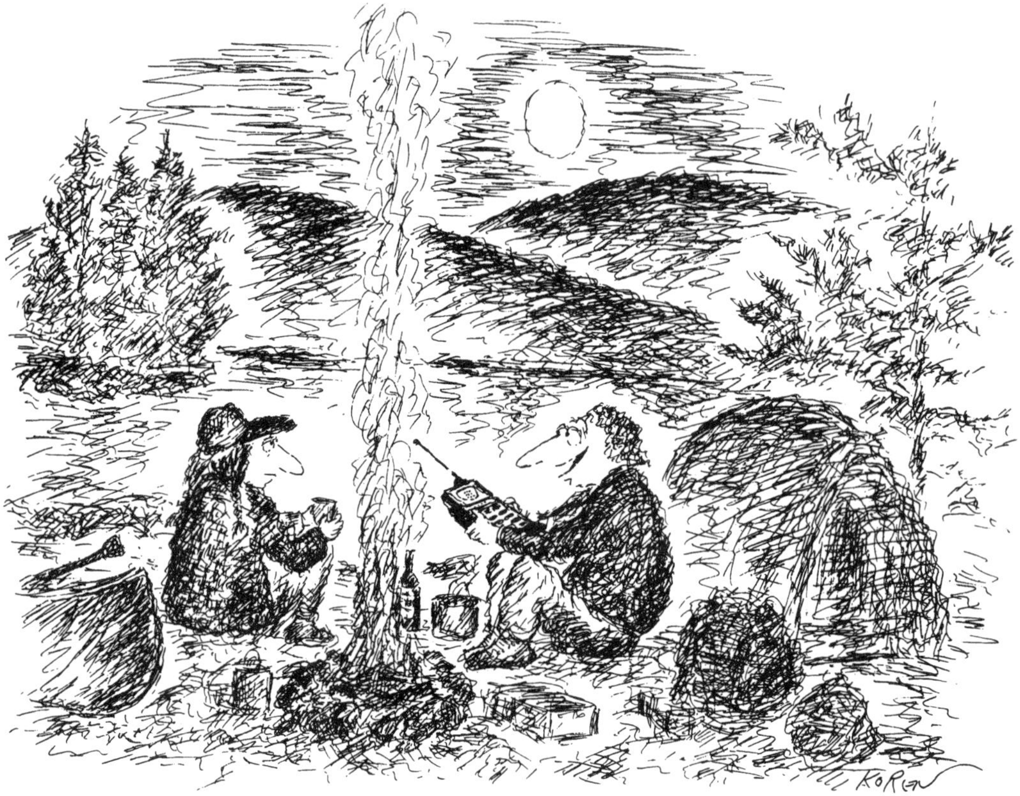
KOREN

"Who can we call?"

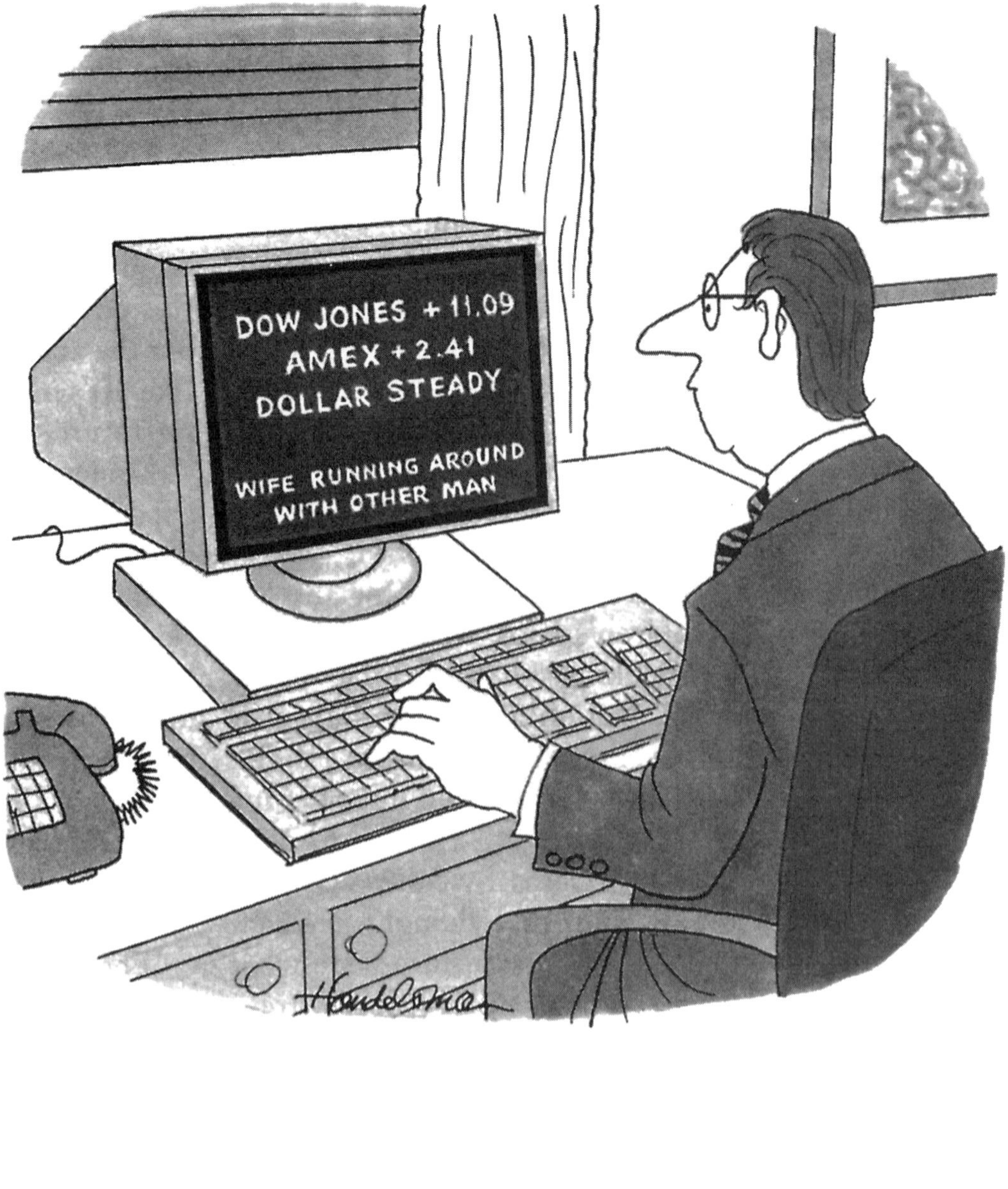
DOW JONES + 11.09
AMEX + 2.41
DOLLAR STEADY
WIFE RUNNING AROUND
WITH OTHER MAN
Handelsman

"We can pause, Stu—we can even try fast-forwarding—
but we can never rewind."

"My God, there's been a terrible accident in our Chicago office!"

"Forgive me, Doris, but some computer hacker from Roslyn, Long Island, has just gained access to my feelings."

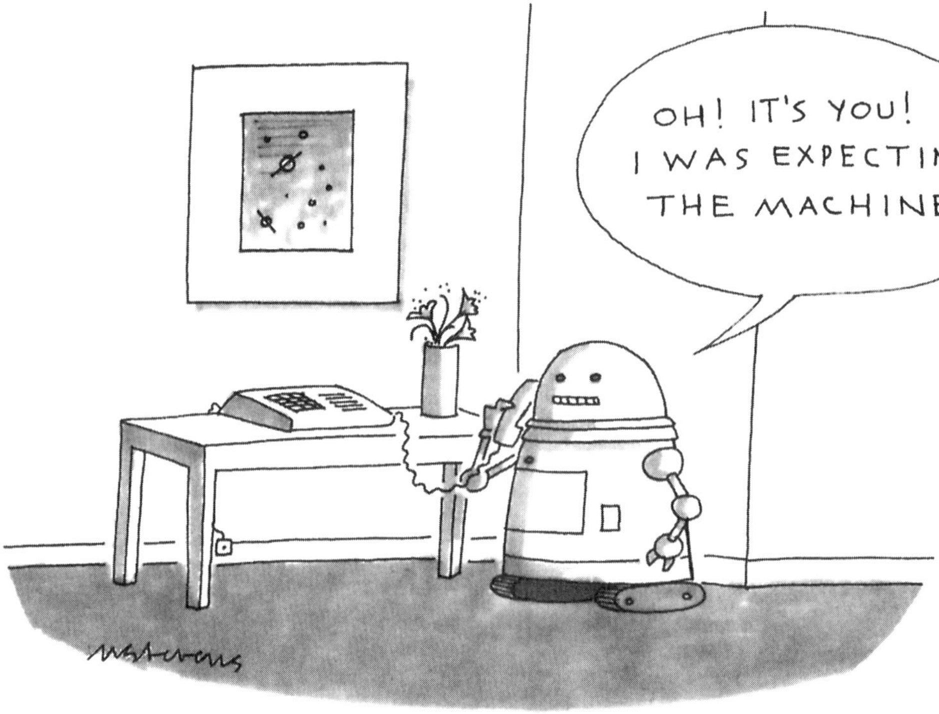
OH! IT'S YOU!
I WAS EXPECTING
THE MACHINE.

"Do we tip it?"

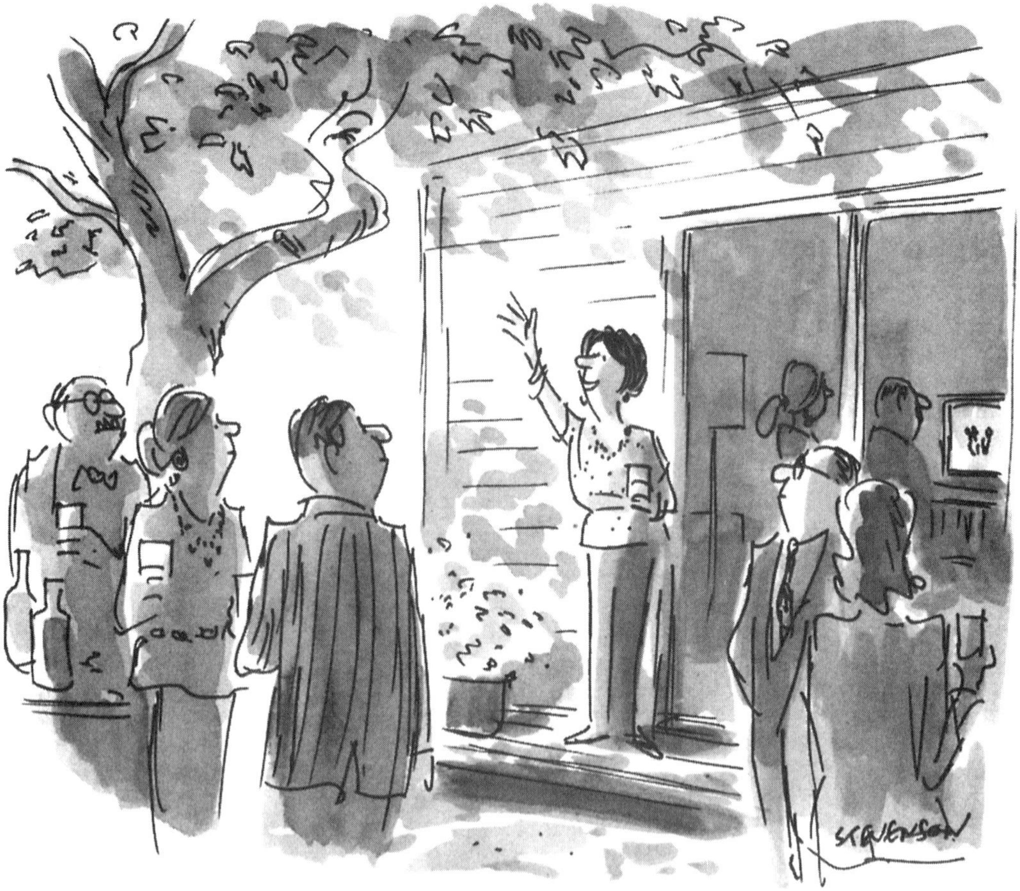
STEVENSON

"Everybody in! We have videotapes of the first hour of the party!"

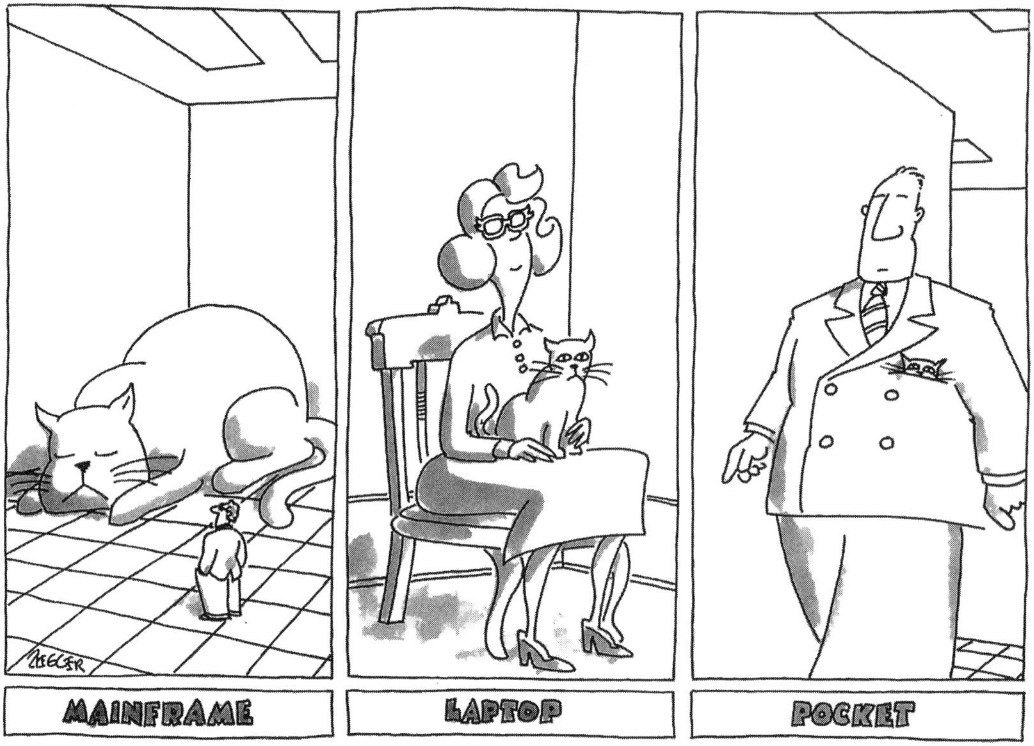
ZIEGLER
MAINFRAME
LAPTOP
POCKET

THE COMPLETE CYCLE

p. Chast

"I think you're looking for 3-D."

"Already my computer is outmoded, but I try to tell myself that my computer isn't <u>me</u>."

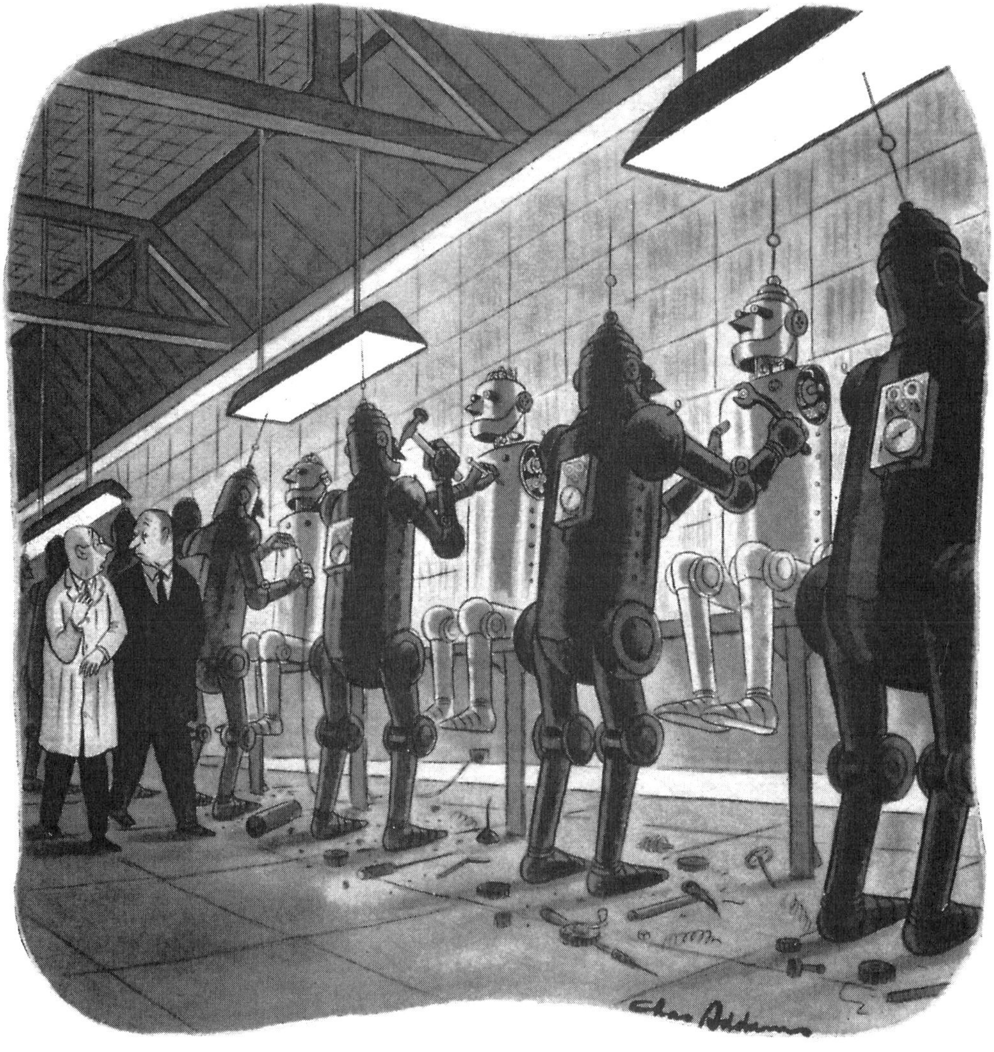
Chas Addams

"Sometimes I ask myself, 'Where will it ever end?'"

"Dennis, I would like to talk to you for a minute—off-line."

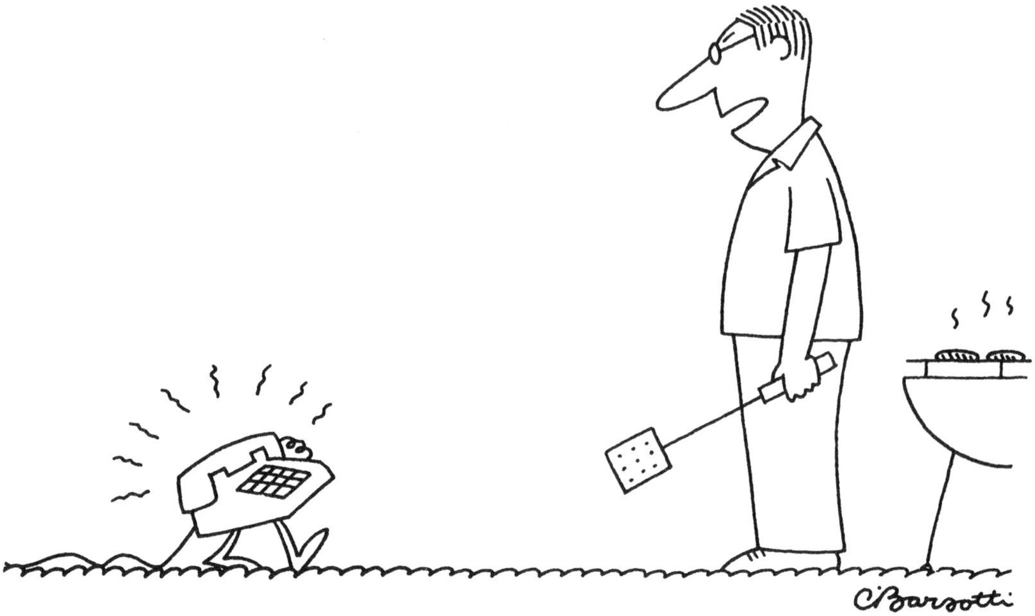

C Barsotti

"What the hell sort of convenient new feature is this?"

McGEVER.

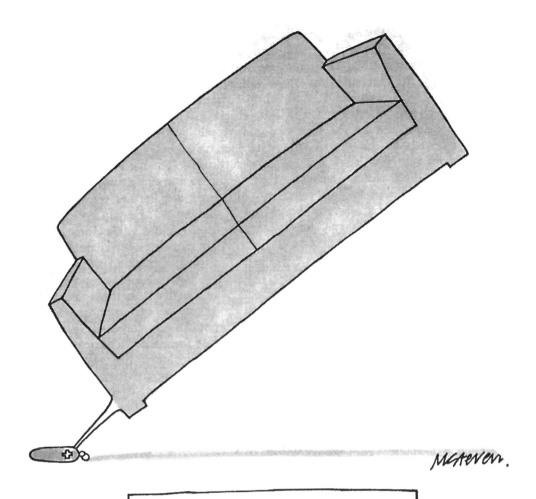

SWISS ARMY COUCH

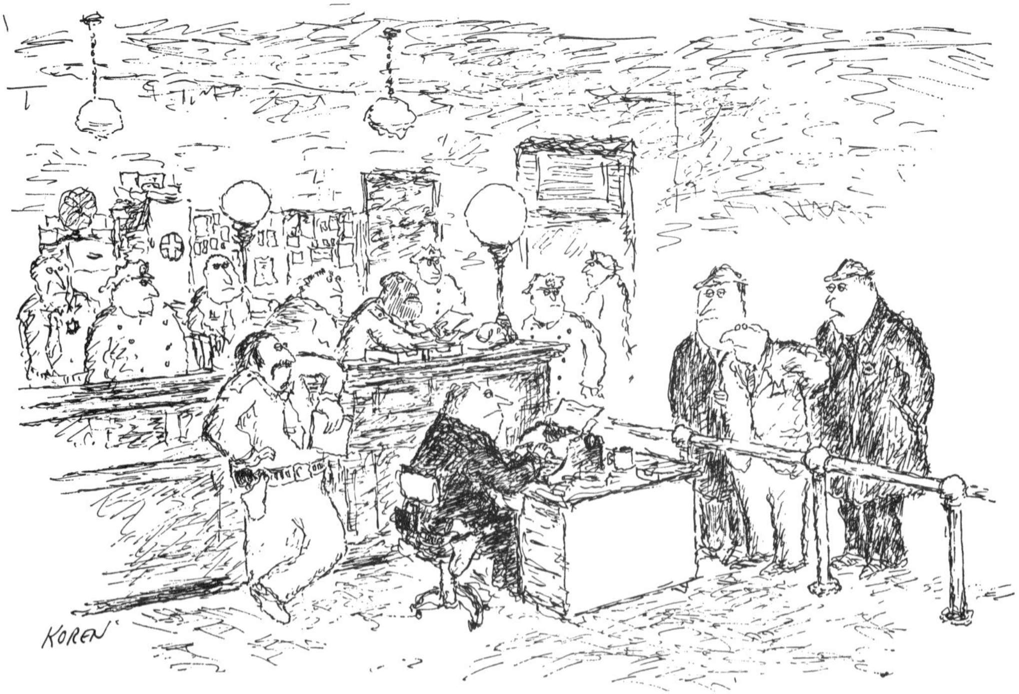
KOREN

"He's charged with expressing contempt for data-processing."

"I just realized, Howard, that everything in this apartment
is more sophisticated than we are."

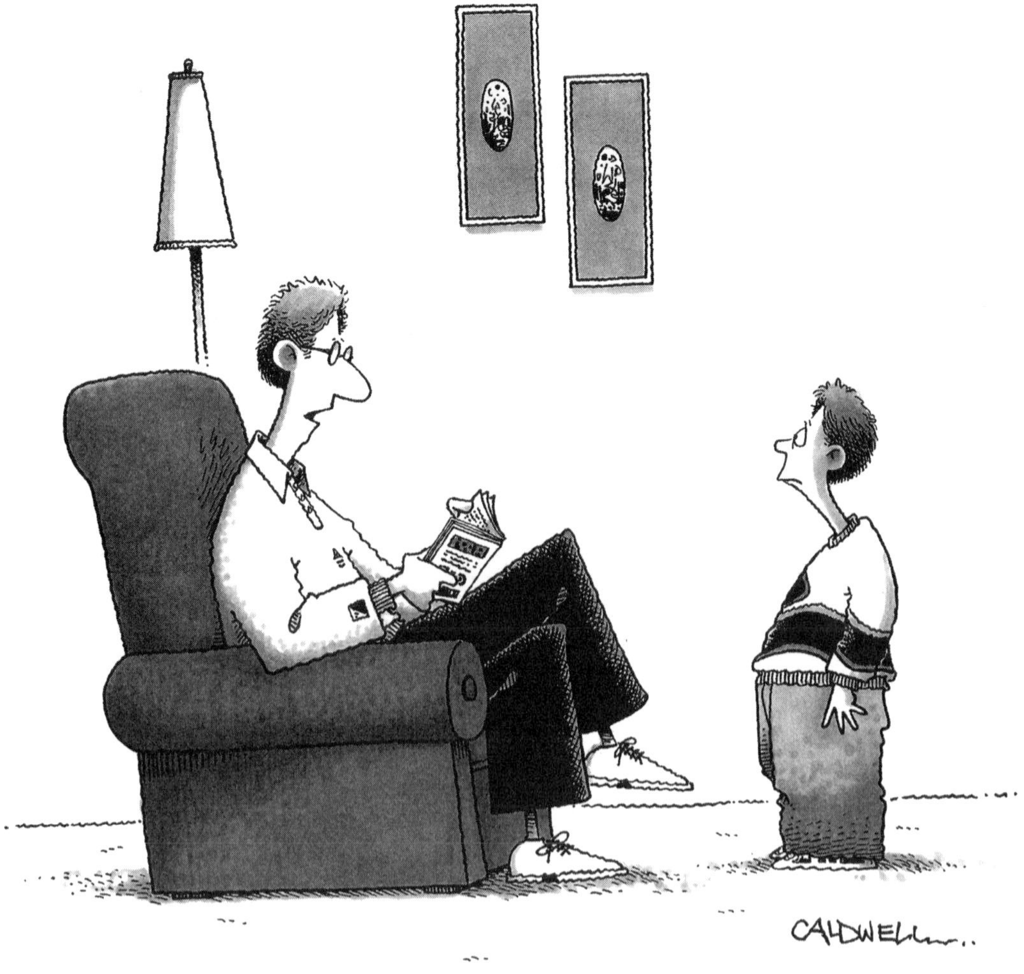
CALDWELL

"Go ask your search engine."

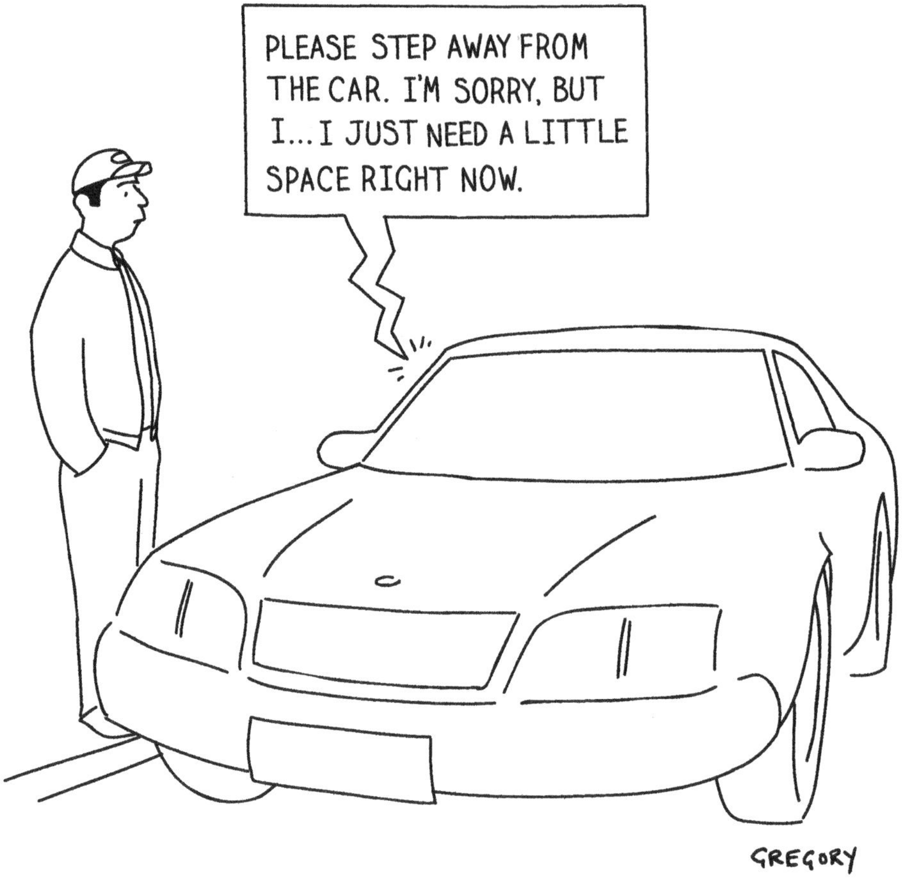
PLEASE STEP AWAY FROM THE CAR. I'M SORRY, BUT I... I JUST NEED A LITTLE SPACE RIGHT NOW.
GREGORY

OVERSENSITIVE CAR ALARM

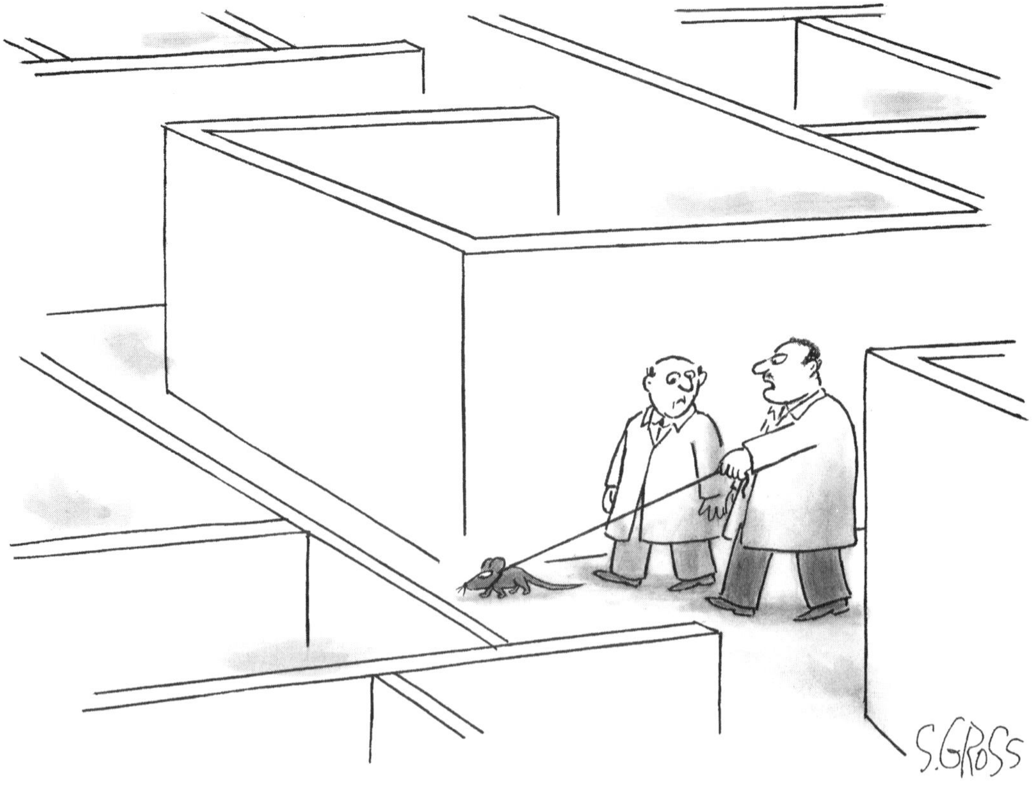
S.GROSS

"Genetic engineering got us into this mess, and genetic engineering will get us out of it."

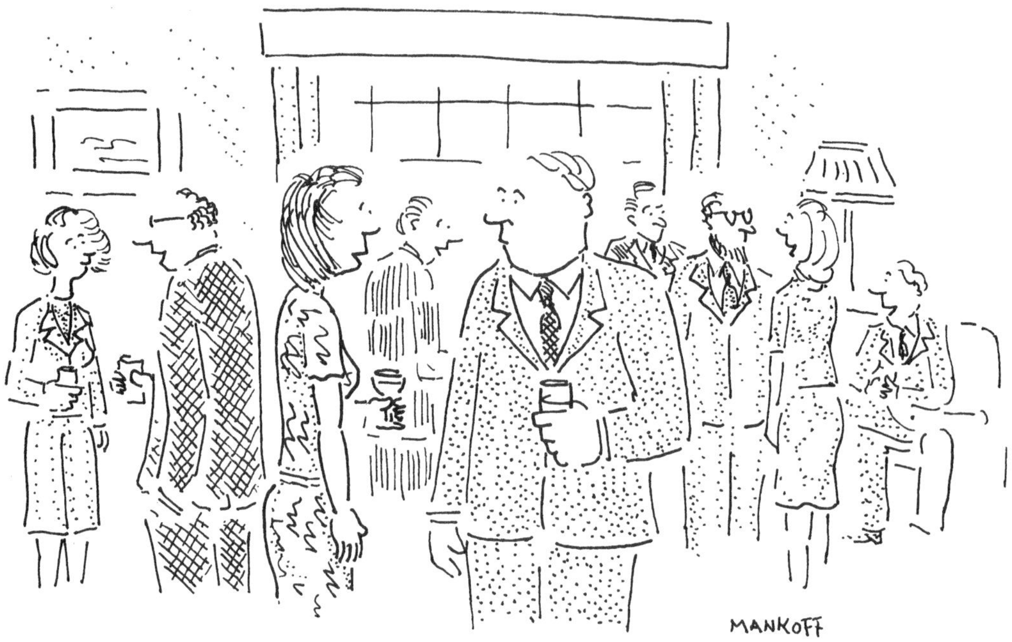
MANKOFF

"I haven't read it yet, but I've downloaded it from the Internet."

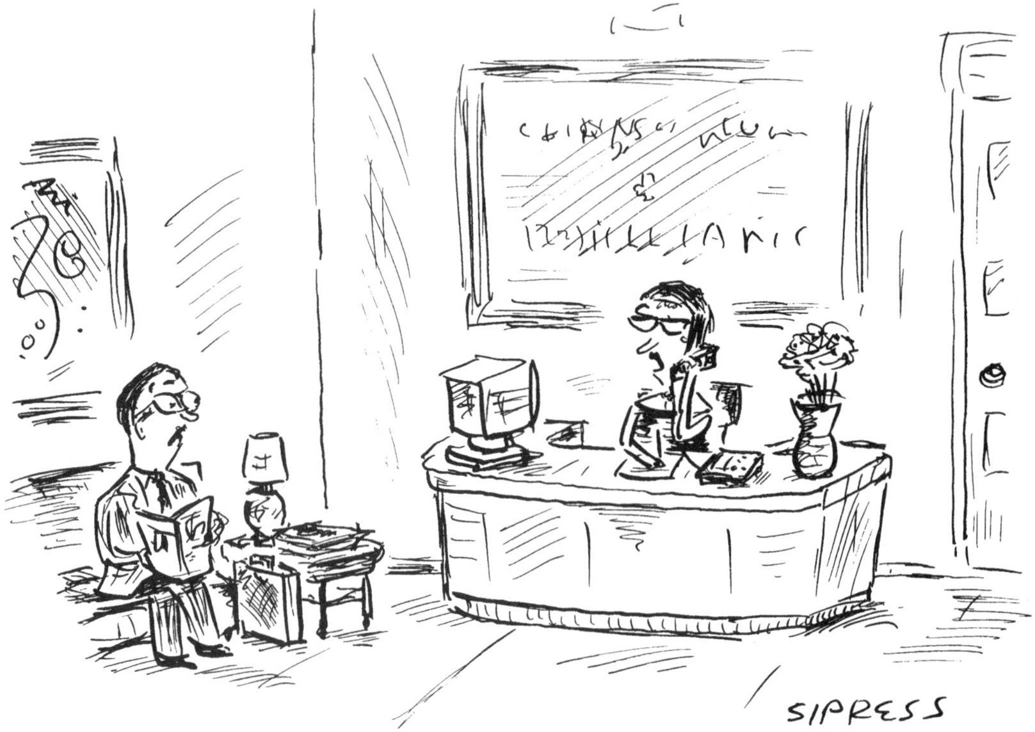
SIPRESS

"He's dead. Would you like his voice mail?"

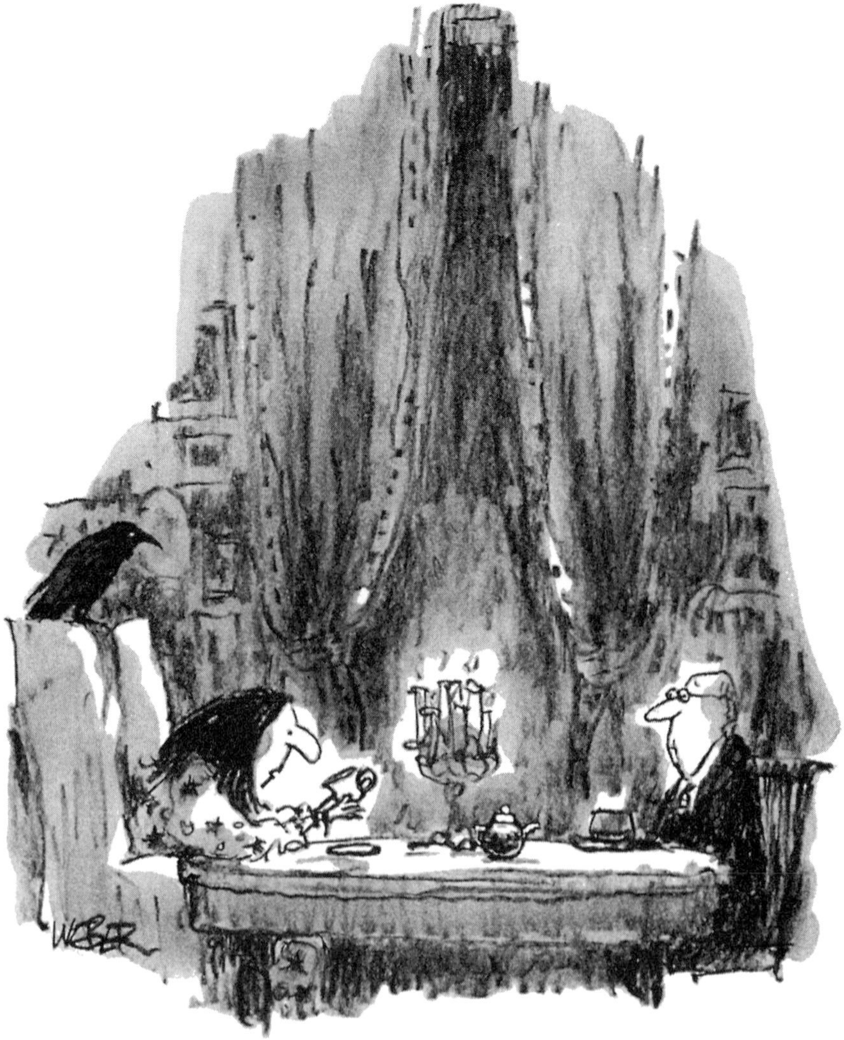
WEBER

"You will never catch up with the new technology."

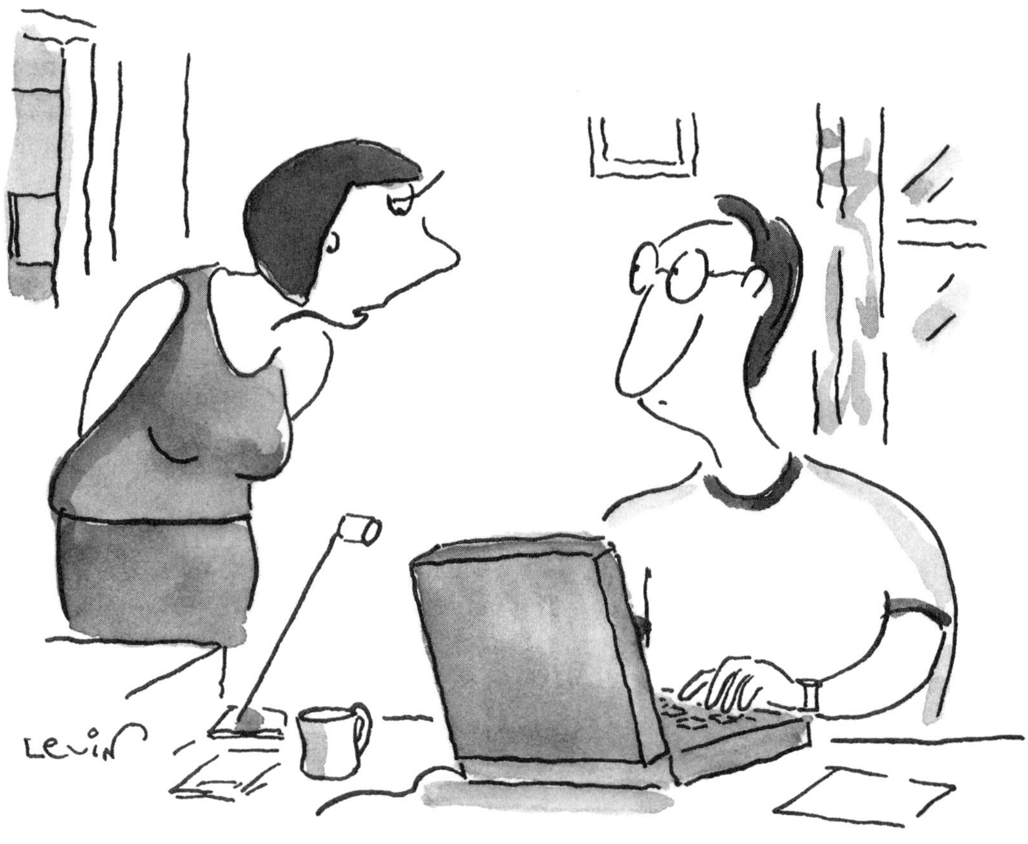
LEVIN

"And just what was that little window you clicked off when I came in?"

CASH MACHINES *from* ACROSS THE LAND

The Big Purse
East Lubbock, New Jersey

Dad's Pocket Casheteria
Twelve Buckets, Nebraska

The Weeping Bankbook
Hensteeth, Alabama

Mattress o' Moola
Knorl, Idaho

R. Chast

"*If you require immediate assistance, press the pound sign.*"

"No, the computers are up. We're down."

COMPUTER
ERROR
ZIEGLER

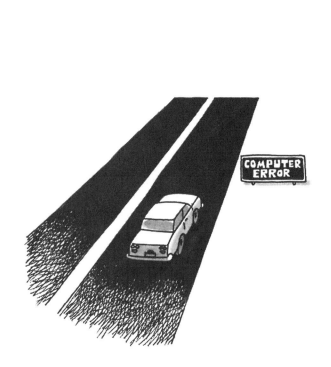

"*I only draw with software.*"

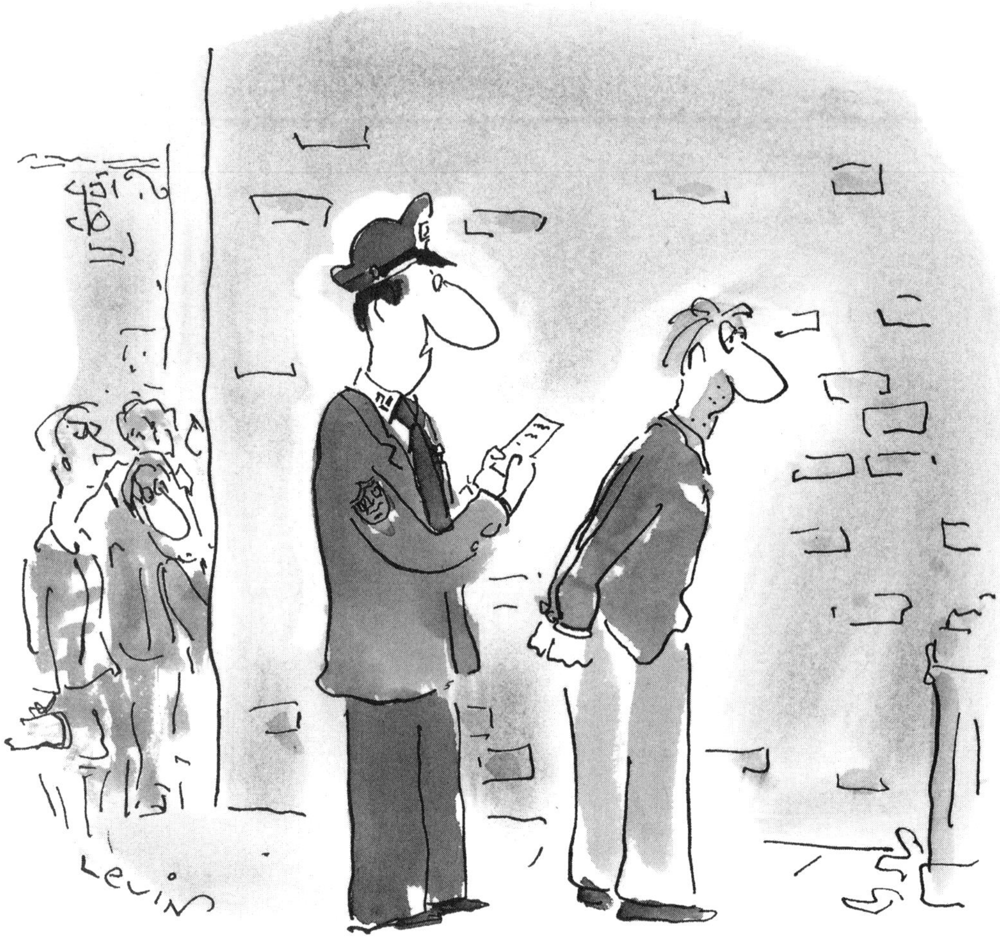
LEVIN

"You have the right to remain silent. Anything you say may be used against you in a court of law, newspapers, periodicals, radio, television, all electronic media, and technologies yet to be invented."

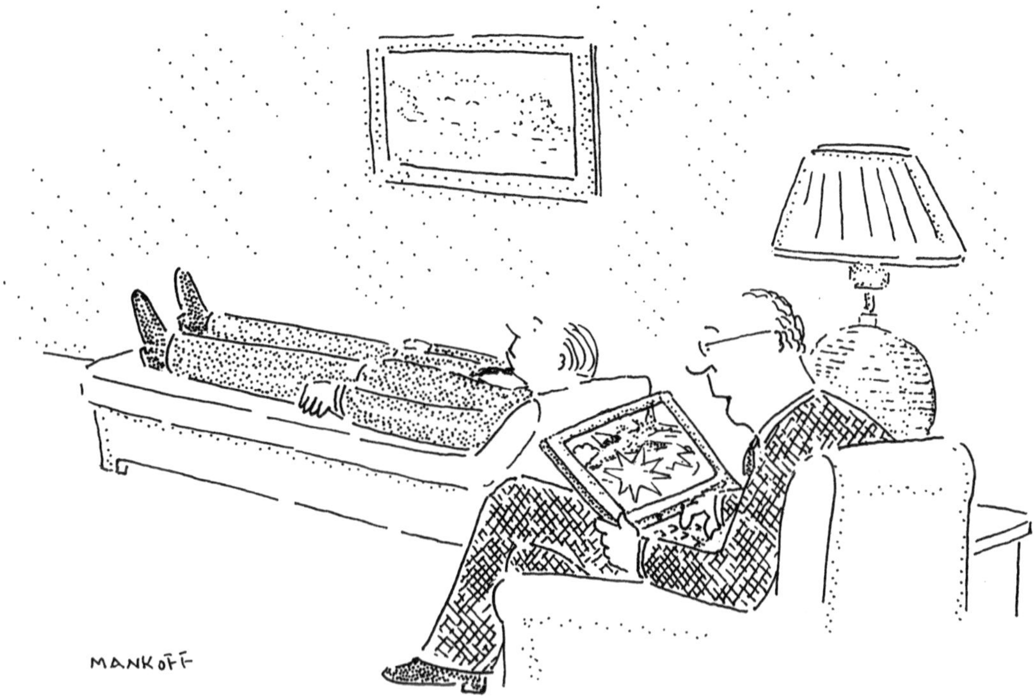
MANKOFF

"You think you have problems? My entire wing command was just destroyed."

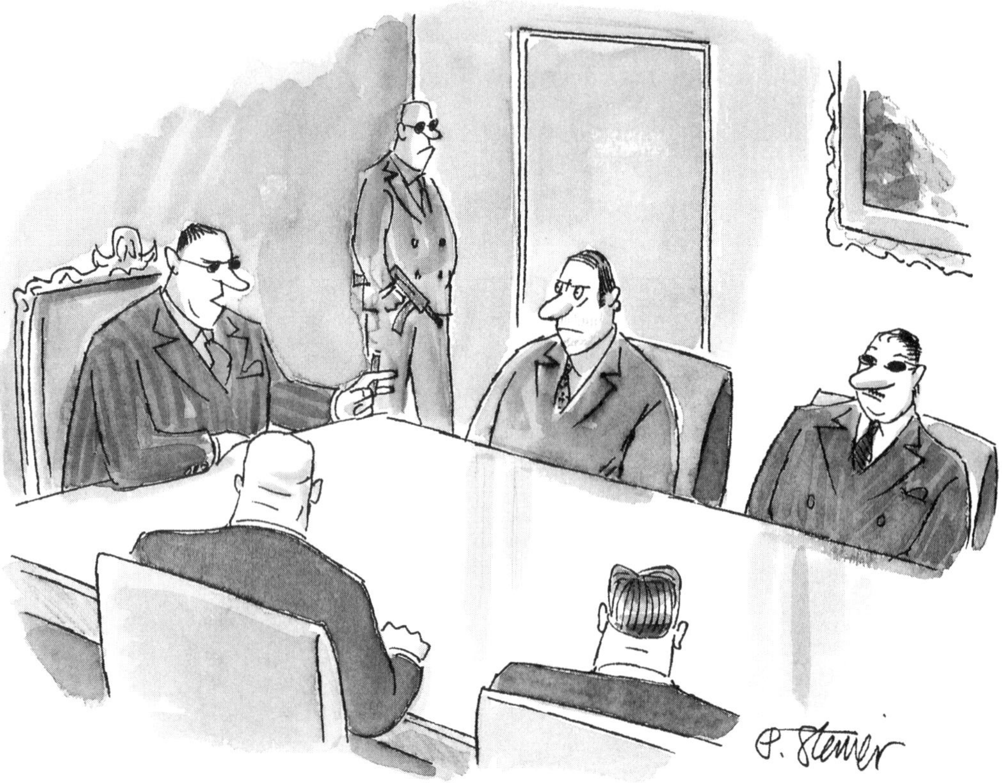
P. Steiner

"Big Tony's Web site—get rid of it."

INDEX OF ARTISTS

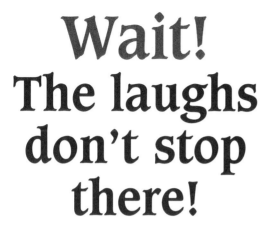

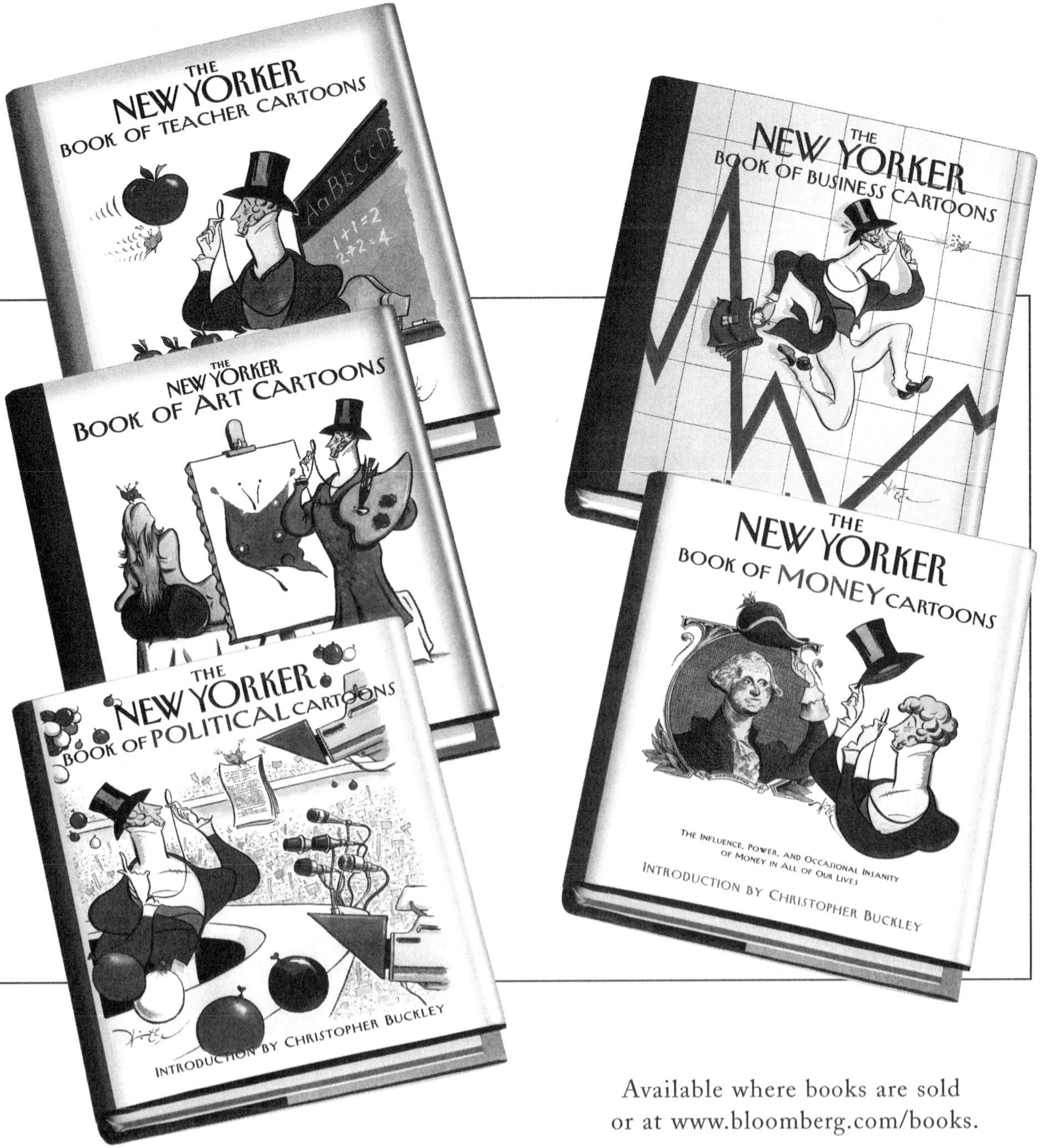
THE NEW YORKER BOOK OF TEACHER CARTOONS
THE NEW YORKER BOOK OF ART CARTOONS
THE NEW YORKER BOOK OF POLITICAL CARTOONS
INTRODUCTION BY CHRISTOPHER BUCKLEY
THE NEW YORKER BOOK OF BUSINESS CARTOONS
THE NEW YORKER BOOK OF MONEY CARTOONS
THE INFLUENCE, POWER, AND OCCASIONAL INSANITY OF MONEY IN ALL OF OUR LIVES
INTRODUCTION BY CHRISTOPHER BUCKLEY